MW00625799

More Praise for
LIFE LESSONS

"This wonderful book will inspire you to set bigger goals than ever before, and motivate you to take continuous action until you succeed."

BRIAN TRACY, AUTHOR OF
NO EXCUSES: THE POWER OF SELF-DISCIPLINE

"Brian Bartes has written a wonderful book that every child who aspires to a better life <u>must</u> own. His guide to successful living is exactly what we adults also need to inspire ourselves to be our children's best role models."

CHERIE CARTER-SCOTT, PH.D., AUTHOR OF
IF LIFE IS A GAME, THESE ARE THE RULES

"*Life Lessons* is loaded with solid wisdom and practical advice with great stories that illustrate the teachings. We can all benefit from learning, or being reminded of, the proven principles of living a balanced, authentic and happy life. Brian Bartes covers the bases well with a clear, easy-to-understand and friendly style. You're going to love it!"

MICHAEL E. ANGIER, FOUNDER OF SUCCESSNET.ORG
AUTHOR OF *101 BEST WAYS TO BE YOUR BEST*
AND *101 BEST WAYS TO GET AHEAD*

"If you want to achieve your potential fast, then get this book! Brian makes it easy with his unique blueprint for creating the life you want."

STEPHANIE FRANK, BEST-SELLING AUTHOR,
THE ACCIDENTAL MILLIONAIRE
WWW.STEPHANIEFRANK.COM

"*Life Lessons* is a valuable addition to my success library at home. It is packed with good advice and illustrations that will educate and inspire readers of all ages. Give it a careful read."

"Brian Bartes writes about the tremendously important lessons in life. His insightful book will inspire anyone who wants to succeed in every area of life, and achieve their dreams."

"I've read over 1,437 books on creating more success in your life. Brian Bartes's new book, *Life Lessons,* is a valuable guide on how to create an outstanding life. I love the inspirational stories in every chapter and the simple to understand and apply action exercises. If you want to create more happiness, success and fun in your life, then read this book. And if you want your children to have the best life possible, give them a copy as well."

"Every great thought leader throughout history has taught us that wisdom is learning from other people's experiences, as well as our own, in order to handle those road bumps with less stress and greater ease. How awesome that Brian Bartes did this with his book, *Life Lessons*! What a great gift for anyone you love. What a great gift for yourself!! What a powerful message for all of us!!"

"Brian Bartes beautifully combines two of my favorite things in *Life Lessons*—real life examples, and stories interwoven with practical and relevant lessons on creating a life that emulates your dreams. Continuing in his usual style Brian provides a fantastic read for those of us who are young, or just young at heart."

KIRSTY DUNPHEY, AUTHOR OF *RETIRED AT 27—*
IF I CAN DO IT, ANYONE CAN
WWW.KIRSTYDUNPHEY.COM

"I believe in Brian Bartes and his new book, *Life Lessons*. There is no better time than NOW to apply Brian's simple genius."

FRANK MCKINNEY, 5X BESTSELLING AUTHOR, INCLUDING *THE TAP*
WWW.FRANK-MCKINNEY.COM

"Brian picked the most important lessons in life, focusing on the ones that make it truly great. Anyone can learn a lot from his guidance and insights."

MICHAEL SLIWINSKI, FOUNDER OF NOZBE;
EDITOR, *PRODUCTIVE!* MAGAZINE

"The best gift a parent can give their child is to help them discover what their unique gift or talent is, and then guide them towards using that gift to benefit humanity. Giving your child *Life Lessons* by Brian Bartes is the perfect way to accomplish this."

ERIN A. KURT, B.ED. AUTHOR OF *JUGGLING FAMILY LIFE:*
A STEP-BY-STEP TO STRESS-FREE PARENTING

"Brian Bartes's masterpiece, *Life Lessons: A Guide to Creating and Living Your Best Life*, is a must-read for everyone. It is a refreshing reminder that work, vision, and execution still produce success even in challenging times. *Life Lessons* is a powerful resource that will help change your life."

LES BROWN, WORLD RENOWNED MOTIVATIONAL SPEAKER

"The principles Brian Bartes shares in *Life Lessons* will change your life. These easy to understand lessons will put you on the right track to living a successful life."

"*Life Lessons* has the power to change the life of any reader who implements its inspirational and practical suggestions. Chock full of inspirational quotes, real life examples, practical suggestions and helpful summaries, Brian's new book presents his insightful blueprint for a successful life!"

"Bravo! Every now and again I read a book that forever impacts my future. *Life Lessons: A Guide to Creating and Living Your Best Life* is one of those books. Read and study this book and not only will you achieve your destiny, but you will also soar in life!"

"Brian gets it! Start now getting the life you want now with Brian's ideas. Life is too short not to!"

"I love books that inspire and motivate people in a positive way, and *Life Lessons* is one of those books."

"*Life Lessons: A Guide to Creating and Living Your Best Life* is an important book to read both for you and your children. In today's world we need important principles for success, and this book will help you to move in the direction of your dreams and make a positive impact in the world. Truth is, we need positive influences to give us the hope and inspiration to be our best. I highly recommend Brian's book."

LEE MILTEER, AUTHOR OF *SUCCESS IS AN INSIDE JOB*
AND *SPIRITUAL POWER TOOLS*
WWW.MILTEER.COM

"*Life Lessons* is a powerful book that can help you achieve your goals in life. Read what Brian Bartes has to say because it can change your life . . . starting today!"

ROBERT STUBERG, AUTHOR OF *THE 12 LIFE SECRETS*

"Brian Bartes presents a proven, easy-to-follow formula for achieving the 'GOOD LIFE,' whatever that may mean to you. Read, reread, digest, and practice the techniques that Brian shares in these great *Life Lessons* and you will Create and Live Your Best Life!"

ED FOREMAN
U. S. CONGRESSMAN, RTD.
(TEXAS AND NEW MEXICO)
SPEAKER, AUTHOR, ENTREPRENEUR

"If you're looking for a great book on how to live your life, you don't have to look any further. I strongly encourage you to read *Life Lessons*."

PEGGY MCCOLL, NEW YORK TIMES BEST-SELLING AUTHOR
WWW.DESTINIES.COM

"*Life Lessons* provides a simple, powerful plan for living a full and successful life."

MARK SANBORN, AUTHOR OF *THE FRED FACTOR* AND
YOU DON'T NEED A TITLE TO BE A LEADER

"Brian Bartes's new book, *Life Lessons*, will inspire a generation of young people to dream big and follow his excellent principles on how to succeed in life. A valuable tool that will have a great influence for all who read and follow his wisdom."

WYLAND, PREMIER OCEAN ARTIST

"Finally, Brian Bartes reveals his keys to success. If you want to make your dreams come true, then read *Life Lessons*!"

MARCIA WIEDER, CEO/FOUNDER, DREAM UNIVERSITY

"Timeless lessons can be taught in new, powerful ways. Brian Bartes does this and more. Read his book and create value for your entire family."

ROBERT WHITE, EXECUTIVE COACH AND
AUTHOR OF *LIVING AN EXTRAORDINARY LIFE*

"*Life Lessons* is filled with inspirational stories, quotes, and strategies for successful living. Read it today, and give a copy to the teenagers and young adults in your life!"

MAC ANDERSON
FOUNDER OF *SIMPLE TRUTHS* AND *SUCCESSORIES*

"If you're ready to live your best life, then read, absorb and use the principles in this book. Brian is giving you a road map for success!"

JAMES MALINCHAK, FEATURED ON
ABC'S HIT TV SHOW, "SECRET MILLIONAIRE"
FOUNDER, WWW.BIGMONEYSPEAKER.COM

To read more praise for *Life Lessons*, visit:
www.lifelessonsthebook.com

LIFE LESSONS

A Guide to Creating and Living Your Best Life

Other Books by Brian Bartes:

Coach Yourself to Success

LifeExcellence Treasury of Quotes

Peace of Mind For You And Your Loved Ones

Co-Authored Books:

Success Simplified

Building an Extraordinary Business

LIFE
LESSONS

A Guide to Creating and Living Your Best Life

BRIAN E.
BARTES

LEGACY PUBLISHING GROUP
Plymouth, Michigan

www.lifelessonsthebook.com

Legacy Publishing Group
P.O. Box 700424
Plymouth, MI 48170
Tel: (734) 254-9970
Fax: (734) 254-9973
www.legacypublishers.com

Ordering Information
Special discounts are available on quantity purchases by corporations, associations, and others. For details, contact the publisher at the address above, or via email at *info@legacypublishers.com*.

Design by 1106 Design, Phoenix, Arizona

Publisher's Cataloging-in-Publication
(Provided by Quality Books, Inc.)

Bartes, Brian E.
    Life lessons : a guide to creating and living your
best life / Brian E. Bartes.
    p. cm.
    ISBN-13: 978-0-9-776773-2-0
    ISBN-10: 0-9776773-2-X

    1. Success. 2. Conduct of life. I. Title.

BF637.S8B37 2011   158.1
                                QBI11-600085

With thanks to everyone who has positively impacted my life. Especially my children—Andy, Abby, Carly, and Caleb—who are my greatest contribution to the world. I hope I have made as much of a difference in their lives as they have made in mine.

CONTENTS

FOREWORD

When Brian Bartes asked me to write the foreword to this book, I was both honored and excited. I often speak to audiences about success, making the most of your life, finding balance and giving back, and have written a number of best sellers with these messages. So Brian and I clearly speak the same language. As I read the manuscript for *Life Lessons,* I realized the application of the lessons Brian shares, combined with enthusiasm and a positive attitude, have made all the difference in my career, and in my life.

My career in TV journalism began in the '70s—a time when there were only a handful of women on news programs. As a senior in college, still contemplating what to do with my life, a family friend said television stations were being pressured by the FCC to put women on their newscasts. I called the News Director, and was soon working as a full-time intern.

As I look back on my career, making that call was the most important thing I did, and it's a key trait in most successful people I've interviewed. They don't wait for good things to happen, they seize opportunities and they make their own success! If you wait around for something great to happen, you could wait a lifetime.

I approached that first job with enthusiasm, a "key ingredient" in turning an opportunity into a success story. I got a lot of people coffee during that time, but I also made myself so valuable in the newsroom that when bigger opportunities came along, I was well positioned to take advantage of them. You have to be willing to say yes to opportunities, to venture out of your comfort zone and take some risks. Over time, the opportunities I said yes to would include local assignments as a weather girl, consumer reporter, news anchor and street reporter, and eventually co-host of *Good Morning America*.

People often ask me, "What was the hardest part of doing *Good Morning America* for 20 years?" I think the biggest challenge was to consistently project—day in and day out—a positive attitude and an exuberance for the day no matter what was happening in my life. I knew that my enthusiasm and my attitude was the first thing the viewer would be exposed to, even prior to the information I had to deliver.

A positive attitude has a tremendous impact on others, but it also has a powerful impact on you. The most important opinion you can possibly have is the one you have of yourself, and the most important things you say all day long are those things you say to yourself. I truly believe that my positive attitude and my enthusiasm for life have been key elements in helping me get to the top of my profession and making it enjoyable along the way.

Brian is very excited to share *Life Lessons* with you. There is always such a need for inspiration in this world of ours, and you will be inspired by the lessons he shares. You will find amazing, real-life stories of those who dared to dream big and stay the course, despite doubters or adversity. I trust that you will enjoy and benefit from reading this book, just as I did, and I hope you will use it to create and live your best life.

Interestingly, much of my success today revolves around health, home and family. All those "little stories" that I learned in my early days have helped shape every area of my life. I hope they have that same effect on you.

JOAN LUNDEN
Television journalist, best-selling author, motivational speaker, and entrepreneur

ACKNOWLEDGMENTS

It has been said that one learns something the best by teaching it. The research, writing, and editing of this book has enabled me to learn anew the life lessons contained herein.

I am eternally grateful for everyone whose efforts have enabled me to share this book with you:

All my mentors—including Jim Bonahoom, John Maxwell, Jim Rohn, and Brian Tracy—for teaching me their best lessons about business and life.

Dawn Dugan, who labored throughout the project, and without whom this book would not have been written.

My special friends who reviewed the book—Beth Anctil, Marti Cowman, Dave Dahlin, Cheryl Geesey, Amy Gillard, Michael Miller, and Bob Smith. They read what I thought was a pretty good book already, and constantly challenged me to improve it. *Life Lessons* is better because of their involvement.

Allyson Aabram, Suzi Deal, Michele DeFilippo, Kris Dulapa, and Ronda Rawlins, for their help at various stages of the project.

Joan Lunden, for believing in the project, and for her Foreword to this book.

And last, but not least, my wife Heidi, for her patience and support while I worked on the book, and her helpful suggestions along the way.

INTRODUCTION

I have studied success my entire adult life. In the last 25 years, I have read hundreds of books and articles about people who have achieved greatness as inventors, artists, scientists, businesspeople, entertainers, and athletes. I have personally met and learned from Super Bowl champions, Olympic athletes, billionaire businessmen, Hollywood actors, and others who have reached the pinnacle of their professions.

My models for success aren't limited to people whose names you would recognize, because many of life's greatest inspirations are neither rich nor famous. They are seemingly ordinary people who are have achieved great personal success in their marriages, or as parents, or serving others in a variety of ways. I continue to observe and learn how people create success, in every area of life.

Everyone loves a good secret, and I am constantly on the lookout for "secrets to success." I suspect that you, too, would enjoy and appreciate the opportunity to learn these "secrets." The fact is, while infomercials, magazines, and marketing campaigns would have us believe otherwise, there are no secrets to success. If you're looking for a magic pill—something that can be quickly obtained and easily applied in order to create immediate success—you won't find it here. Or anywhere.

What I can offer you is this: While there are no "secrets to success," there *are* certain immutable principles—"life lessons" if you will. This book is a compilation of those principles. By learning and applying the lessons contained in this book, you will greatly increase your likelihood of achieving success, however you define it.

Life Lessons is written for two groups of people. The first group is children, who are the future of the world. This book started out as a way to gather in one place the most important lessons I wanted my own children to learn. I hope you will be inspired to give this book to your children, and to the high school and college graduates in your life—that they will learn, embrace and apply these lessons, and that their lives will be better for having done so.

As much as *Life Lessons* started out as a book for young people, I realize that it also provides an opportunity for adults to learn these important principles for success. It is never too early to start learning these lessons, and it is never too late to begin applying them in your own life.

As you read *Life Lessons*, I hope it will move you to create greater success in your life, and that your actions will make a positive impact in the world.

BRIAN BARTES

SECTION I
LIFE LESSONS

"These motivation tapes have really inspired me!
I'm going to make a million dollars, buy my own company
and retire early. Then I'm going to write a screenplay,
cure a disease and give all the profits to charity.
And tomorrow I'll do even MORE!"

CHAPTER 1

DREAM BIG DREAMS

Cherish your visions and your dreams,
as they are the children of your soul—the
blueprints of your ultimate achievements.
—NAPOLEON HILL

A CELL PHONE SALESMAN SINGS OPERA

It was March 17, 2007. Simon Cowell's new show, *Britain's Got Talent,* was holding auditions at the Wales Millennium Centre in Cardiff, Wales. Paul Potts, a 36-year-old cell phone salesman, strolled awkwardly onto the stage.

He stepped in front of the microphone, and stood nervously in the cheap suit he had just purchased for the audition. His appearance was further diminished by the sight of a chipped tooth, which was damaged in a childhood accident.

When he announced to the judges that he was going to sing opera, their eyes rolled in disbelief. Based on what they had seen so far, the judges and audience undoubtedly thought Potts was about to make a fool of himself. In fact, even Potts seemed to doubt his ability. After all, his only experience had been singing in the school and church choirs when he was younger. Later, he would state that being bullied in school probably had an influence on his lack of self-confidence.

> *The great thing in this world is not so much where we stand as in what direction we are moving.*
>
> —Oliver Wendell Holmes

Then the tenor from south Wales opened his mouth, and started to sing. Just 10 seconds into Giacomo Puccini's "Nessun Dorma," everyone knew they were listening to something quite extraordinary. Within 20 seconds, the audience of 2,000 began cheering loudly. By the end of the performance, many in the audience (and one of the judges) had been brought to tears by the amazing performance they had just witnessed. Potts received a standing ovation.

"Simply magical," said Simon Cowell. "Incredible," agreed fellow judge Piers Morgan. The third judge, Amanda Holden, was moved to tears, and said his voice had left her covered in goosebumps. "We were not expecting that," said Cowell.

Potts went on to win *Britain's Got Talent,* and performed later that year at the *Royal Variety Performance,* in front of Queen Elizabeth.

"By day, I sell mobile phones," said Paul Potts. "My dream is to spend my life doing what I feel that I was born to do . . . to sing opera."

A BILLION SERVINGS OF CHICKEN SOUP

Mark Victor Hansen and Jack Canfield already had successful careers when their first *Chicken Soup for the Soul* book was published in 1983. Part of their early success in selling and professional speaking was due to the inspirational and motivational stories they would tell. By the time they gathered the collection of 101 stories that would comprise their first book, Hansen and Canfield had already created big dreams for *Chicken Soup for the Soul.*

> *As long as you're going to be thinking anyway,*
> *THINK BIG.*
> —*Donald Trump*

Their initial dream was to sell 150,000 copies the first year and 1 million copies the second year. They hoped to create a book that would make a huge difference in the world. But they far surpassed that dream. Before long, they had dozens of titles, and had sold over 50 million books.

Rather than resting on their laurels, they decided to create a bigger dream. They are now on a mission to sell one billion *Chicken Soup for the Soul* books. So far, there are almost 200 *Chicken Soup* titles with more than 112 million books sold in more than 40 languages!

Hansen and Canfield wrote in *Chicken Soup for the Soul: Living Your Dreams:* "We have learned that as soon as you commit to a big dream and really go after it, not only will your creative mind come up with big ideas to make it happen, you will also start attracting the people you need in your life to make your dream come true."

IT ALL BEGAN WITH A MOUSE

Walter Elias Disney grew up on a family farm in Marceline, Missouri. As a young boy, he loved to draw. Though money was tight and the chores needed to be done, his mother and older brother encouraged Walt to pursue his passion. After studying art and photography in high school, he took night classes at the Chicago Art Institute.

Walt's dream was to become an animator and create a cartoon character that he would be remembered by. He based the character on a pet mouse he had while working in Kansas City. Walt named the mouse "Mortimer," but his wife thought the name didn't suit the mouse's character. Walt renamed the character "Mickey Mouse."

Today the name "Walt Disney" is synonymous with cutting-edge animation, award-winning entertainment, and quintessential theme parks. But back then Disney was turned down for jobs and told he lacked talent. Since others wouldn't hire him, Walt started his own company. It soon went bankrupt. With only $20 in his pocket, Walt headed to Hollywood to pursue his dreams.

The rest is history. Walt Disney went on to become one of the largest influences in 20th century entertainment, and one of the most prolific and well-known producers in the world. Disney dared to do what other animators didn't, and as a result became one of the industry's most important innovators.

> *All our dreams can come true, if we have the courage to pursue them.*
> —*Walt Disney*

Walt Disney proved that the largest dreams have no boundaries or timelines, and have the ability to positively impact others long after the dreamer is gone.

And it all started with a mouse . . . and a dream.

It Starts With a Dream

If you ever want to learn about the concept of "dreaming big dreams," talk to a child. For children, no dream seems too big. When asked what they want to be when they grow up, kids say things like "I want to be a fireman," or "I want to be a doctor," or "I'm going to be an astronaut!"

When you talk to children about what they want to do, their responses have no boundaries. "I want to build the world's tallest skyscraper." "I want to eat ice cream on the moon." "I want to dig to China!"

Kids grow up with heroes all around them. Some heroes play sports such as basketball, football, and golf. Others are "superheroes," whose powers are limitless, and who appear larger than life on movie screens and in comic books. Even "ordinary" people are viewed as heroes by children whose parents, teachers, and other mentors have made a positive impact on their lives.

Dreams come a size too big so we can grow into them.

—Author unknown

Children possess a beautiful innocence about the world. A refreshing naiveté of what is truly possible.

Of course, our child-like perception of the world changes as we grow older. Those with good intentions start to "protect" us from the harsh realities of our world today. At first, they explain that our dreams *might not* come true. They mean well as they prepare us for the possibility of failure, and soften the blow of inevitable defeat.

As children grow up, they are advised by those around them to forego goals and dreams that get labeled as "unrealistic" at best, or "impossible" at worst. They are encouraged to pursue a more conservative life path than the one described in their dreams. "Settle down and find a job," they are advised. "Preferably something dependable, with a regular paycheck and health insurance."

All the while, the unsupportive messages seep into their subconscious. They are reinforced by experiences which tend to support the idea that dreaming big dreams is a path to disappointment.

Eventually, most people let their dreams die. They are consoled by others who have traveled down a similar road. Their dreams for the future get tucked into the past, together with their Lego® toys and their astronaut uniform.

Hold Onto Your Dreams

Your dreams are seeds that grow and take on a life of their own. They inspire you to take the actions necessary to make them come true. The more you dream, the more you are inspired. The more inspired you are, the more actions you take. This continues, until one morning you wake up to find that your dream has come true.

Everything great that has ever been accomplished started with a dream. Here are a few examples:

- Katie Couric dreamed of becoming a news anchor. She held onto her dream, even after being pulled off the air by a CNN executive who told her she had no future. After co-hosting the *Today Show* for 15 years, Couric became the first solo female news anchor for a major network's nightly news. She also became the highest paid news anchor at the time, earning a reported $15 million per year.

- Jim Carrey dreamed of being a successful Hollywood movie star. Long before he was famous, Carrey wrote a check to himself for $10 million. On the memo line, he wrote "For Services Rendered." He carried the check in his wallet for years, occasionally pulling it out to remind himself of his dream. Carrey's dream eventually came true, making him one of the highest-paid entertainers in the movie business.

- Mary Kay Ash "envisioned a company in which any woman could become just as successful as she wanted to be. The doors would be wide open to opportunity for women who were willing to pay the price and had the courage to dream." Although Ash sold only $1.50 in products at her first beauty show, she never lost sight of her commitment to making life better for women. Today, Mary Kay® is one of the world leaders in the beauty care industry. More importantly, the company continues to inspire, enrich, and empower women to achieve their potential and bring their dreams to life.

What do all of these people have in common? They dreamed big dreams, and they held onto those dreams until they came true. This is a characteristic common in all great achievement. David McClelland, a Harvard psychologist who has studied high achievers, has concluded that people who are successful have one thing in common: they are constantly dreaming about how to achieve their goals.

> Go confidently in the direction of your dreams. Live the life you have imaged.
> —Henry David Thoreau

Take a few minutes right now to define your dream. Think about what life would be like if you accomplished it. If you don't know where to begin, start by asking yourself these questions:

- If you could be, do, or have anything in the world, what would you want?
- What would you attempt to do if you knew you could not fail?

Commit to Your Dream

In his well-known book on success, *Oh, The Places You'll Go*, Dr. Seuss introduces something he calls "The Waiting Place." This is the place where many people become stuck. They don't have the courage to pursue their dream, because they are afraid of failing. They know they need to do something, but fear and indecision keeps them stuck in neutral. Deep down they think their dreams are unrealistic or silly, or

> *The future belongs to those who believe in the beauty of their dreams.*
> —*Eleanor Roosevelt*

they just don't think they have it in them to do what it takes to succeed.

How do you get out of the waiting place? By fully committing to the pursuit of your dreams. Once you have defined your dream, you must decide that you are going to go for it, and that nothing is going to stop you.

Create an Action Plan

In order to accomplish your dreams, you must develop a step-by-step plan for getting from where you are to where you want to be. Write down everything that will have to happen to make your dream a reality. Here are some things to consider:

- **A timeframe.** How long will it take to realize your dream?
- **Action steps.** What has to be done, and when will you complete each step?
- **Resources.** How will you accomplish each step? Who else needs to be involved? What support structures will need to be in place?

- **Measurement.** The old adage, "what gets measured, gets done" is true. How will you evaluate your progress?

This is the point at which many people put all of this information "in a box" to be taken out at a "more convenient time." Don't be one of those people because, for most of them, that time never comes. Instead of putting this information away, act on it right now. You may have to move outside your comfort zone to take the first few steps, and it's quite likely you'll encounter challenges. Climb over them, go around them, dig under them, or knock them down.

Remember, everyone who accomplished their dreams started right where you are today. If you continue to take action in the direction of your ideal life, you'll eventually realize your dreams.

Encourage Others to Dream Big, Too

It's so easy for people to let their dreams die. It happens all the time, for a variety of reasons. Dreams are easily dismissed by those around us, which can cause people to let their dreams go.

Don't add to this phenomenon. Don't be a naysayer, someone who dampens the dreams of those around you. Instead, encourage others to dream big, too. Talk to those around you about their goals and aspirations.

Ask them questions, listen to their responses, and provide the kind of support that will inspire them in the pursuit of their dream. Your encouragement will not only help them, but it will inspire you, as well.

> *The only place where your dream becomes impossible is in your own thinking.*
> —*Robert H. Schuller*

Here are a few famous people whose encouragement by others made all the difference in their success:

- Marine life artist Wyland was encouraged by his first-grade teacher, who told him he could be a great artist.
- Ray Charles was encouraged by a local pianist named Wylie Pitman to pursue his dream of playing the piano, despite the fact he was blind.
- Babe Ruth was an orphan who was encouraged by the orphanage priest to pursue professional baseball.

Where would we be as a society if these people had not been encouraged by others? When a dream goes unfulfilled, it's a huge loss not only for the dreamer, but for those around them, and perhaps even for the world.

What Is Your Dream?

Neil Armstrong dreamed of landing on the moon. Thomas Edison dreamed of creating a simple and inexpensive source of light. The Wright brothers dreamed of flying a powered machine. Bill Gates dreamed about a computer on every desk and in every home.

What is *your* big dream . . . and what will you do *today* to make it come true?

> *When you want something, all the universe conspires in helping you to achieve it.*
> —*Paulo Coelho*

LIFE LESSONS

✓ Take out a piece of paper, and write down the answer to the following questions: If you could be, do, or have anything in the world, what would you want? What would you attempt to do if you could not fail?

✓ Resolve today that you are going to make your dreams a reality, and that nothing is going to stop you. Write down everything that will have to happen in order for you to make your dreams come true.

✓ What one action can you take today toward realizing your dreams? Whatever your answer, do it now!

For more stories about people who dream big dreams, visit Brian Bartes's *Life Lessons* blog:

www.lifelessonsthebook.com/blog

CHAPTER 2

Always Believe In Yourself

"There is no use in trying," said Alice.
"One can't believe impossible things."
"I dare say you haven't had much practice," said the
Queen. "When I was your age, I always did it for
half an hour a day. Why, sometimes I've believed as
many as six impossible things before breakfast."

—Lewis Carroll, in *Through the Looking Glass*

The Greatest of All Time

Cassius Clay always believed in himself. As a young boy growing up in Louisville, Kentucky, Clay's parents instilled in him a sense of pride and confidence. They taught him that he could be the best at anything he set his mind to. Clay's confidence was displayed frequently in neighborhood games with his friends. Whether playing marbles or in a race to the end of the block, he always believed he would win.

Clay took up boxing in high school, and soon declared that he was going to become heavyweight champion of the world. He boasted weekly, if not daily, to anyone who would listen. When he ran through downtown Louisville as part of his training, he would tell people he was training for the Olympics, and that he was going to win a gold medal. He also let them know that once he returned home from the Olympics, he was going to turn pro and become the heavyweight boxing champion of the world.

> *I'm so fast that last night I turned off the light switch in my hotel room and was in bed before the room was dark.*
>
> *—Muhammad Ali*

Just as he predicted, Clay won a gold medal at the 1960 Summer Olympics in Rome. In 1964, at the age of 22, Clay became the youngest boxer ever to take the heavyweight title from a reigning champ. He changed his name to Muhammad Ali, and then went on to win the world heavyweight boxing championship a record three times.

Ali never thought of failing. He continually focused his thoughts on the fame and glory he would receive when he won. These positive thoughts permeated his thinking, and dominated his life. He believed in himself, declaring that he was "The Greatest of All Time." In 1999, *Sports Illustrated* magazine confirmed Ali's assessment, naming him "Sportsman of the Century."

PURSUING HAPPYNESS

Christopher Gardner sat in his living room, watching a college basketball game with his mother. When the television announcers discussed the promising futures of the young athletes, the 16-year-old's ears suddenly perked up.

"Wow, one day those guys are gonna make a million dollars," said Chris.

"Son," his mother responded, "If you want to, one day *you* could make a million dollars."

Those words stuck with him.

Years later, Gardner found himself struggling to make ends meet as a medical equipment salesperson. In addition to his career demands, he was also doing his best as a single dad trying to raise his two-year-old son. At times, he and his son were homeless, sleeping in shelters and bathrooms of train stations.

As he walked down the street one afternoon, Gardner saw a man get out of a red Ferrari that had just pulled up to the curb. He approached the man, and asked him what he did for a living. "I'm a stockbroker," the man responded.

Despite the fact he had no experience and no connections, Gardner decided that he, too, was going to become a stockbroker. He befriended another stockbroker and talked his way into the rigorous Dean Witter training program. While Gardner was given only a small stipend on which to survive during the training program, he never doubted that he would score well on the licensing exam and be offered a job.

> *To accomplish great things, we must not only act, but also dream; not only plan but also believe.*
>
> —*Anatole France*

Gardner's enormous belief in himself propelled him from homeless father to successful stockbroker. By the age of 34 he had made his first million. He celebrated his success by purchasing a Ferrari formerly owned by Michael Jordan.

Gardner would later write a book documenting his life, called *The Pursuit of Happyness*. His story was eventually turned into a movie starring Will Smith.

BREAKING THE FOUR-MINUTE MILE

They called it the "impossible barrier." No human being had ever run a mile in less than four minutes. More than 50 medical journals had published articles describing this feat as an insurmountable human limitation.

But one man believed. His name was Roger Bannister. On May 6, 1954, in spite of the rain and 15 mile-per-hour crosswind at Oxford University's Iffley Road Track, the

British medical student set a new world record, running the mile in 3 minutes, 59.4 seconds. Not only had Bannister cut a full two seconds off the old world record, but he also ran the world's first sub-four-minute mile.

In recognition of his accomplishment, Bannister received *Sports Illustrated's* first Sportsman of the Year Award in 1954. The magazine compared Bannister's four-minute mile breakthrough with the scaling of Mt. Everest as the most significant athletic feat of the 20th century. In 2005, *Forbes* magazine named Bannister's feat the "greatest athletic achievement of the last 150 years."

Years later, Bannister talked about the belief system that had been created around the four-minute-mile. "There was a mystique, a belief that it couldn't be done, but I think it was more of a psychological barrier than a physical barrier." Bannister refused to believe the conventional wisdom, because he didn't want to limit his own potential.

> *Impossible is just a big word thrown around by small men who find it easier to live in a world they've been given than to explore the power they have to change it. Impossible is not a fact. It is an opinion. Impossible is not a declaration. It's a dare. Impossible is potential. Impossible is temporary. Impossible is nothing.*
>
> —*Adidas ad*

In breaking the four-minute mile, Bannister would pave the way for others to believe, then accomplish, this incredible feat. Just six weeks later, running rival John Landy would match Bannister's accomplishment. The seemingly impossible barrier has since been broken by many runners, including American Steve Scott, who has run the sub-four-minute mile 136 times!

You Must First Believe

All great accomplishment requires belief. If it isn't the most important ingredient for success, it is certainly an essential ingredient. Muhammad Ali recognized this at a very early age. Chris Gardner's mom knew it, and instilled that idea in her son. Roger Bannister also realized that, in order to achieve his seemingly impossible feat, he would first have to *believe* he could do it. And so it is with everyone who has ever accomplished anything great.

> *Everything is possible for him who believes.*
> —Mark 9:23

Think about the great inventions that have changed the world: The printing press, the telephone, modes of transportation such as the automobile and the airplane, the light bulb, television, and the computer. None of these inventions would have been created except for the belief and persistence of their inventors. The same is true of the things *you* want to accomplish.

You were born with the belief that you could do anything. As a young child, you feared nothing. You may have jumped into a pool when you hadn't yet learned to swim. Or tried to climb on something that was far too high for you to be on. The thought never occurred to you that you couldn't do the thing you were attempting.

> *Believe, really believe, you can move a mountain and you can. Not many people believe that they can move mountains. So, as a result, not many people do.*
>
> —David Schwartz

Because your parents' job was to keep you safe during these formative years, you were given limits. You heard words like "no," and phrases such as "don't do that" or "that is *not* okay." You also discovered through your own experience that you couldn't do *everything*. For example, some things were just not possible physically. Guidance from others, coupled with your own experiences, caused you to modify your behavior.

Parents and others mean well, and the phrases and limits described above are usually provided out of love and concern for safety. It's also important to realize that there really are certain physical limits to what we are able to do. You wouldn't want to jump from the roof of your house, for example, thinking that you could fly.

While much of this feedback is constructive, you want to be careful that it doesn't limit your thinking about what *is* possible. If someone repeats over and over again that you can't do something, your belief system tends to change. If you try something several times and things don't go well, it's easy to begin questioning yourself, and what you are able to accomplish.

Conditioned to Believe

Have you ever wondered why the elephants at the circus stand quietly tied to a chain and stake, when they could easily break free? It's because the elephants are tied to a heavy chain and stake when they are young. No matter how hard they try, they are not able to pull themselves free. This continues until they are trained to believe that they can't escape. By the time they are old enough and strong enough to free themselves, they are constrained by their limiting beliefs. As adults, they don't even *try* to break free.

An experiment conducted with fleas teaches us a similar lesson. Fleas are able to jump extremely high. In the experiment, a flea was put into a glass jar, and the lid was placed on the jar. Because the flea could jump higher than the jar, it banged into the lid each time it jumped. The flea jumped over and over again, each time hitting the lid of the jar.

Then, something interesting happened. The flea began jumping almost to the top of the jar, but not quite. Each time the flea jumped, it stopped just short of the lid. In this learned behavior, the flea realized that it could not jump out of the jar, so it stopped trying.

This continued for a while, and then the lid was removed. Guess what happened when they took the lid off? The flea continued to jump just beneath the height of the jar.

Like elephants and fleas, our ability to accomplish our goals is directly tied to what we believe. If you've been told from a very young age that you

Man often becomes what he believes himself to be. If I keep on saying to myself that I cannot do a certain thing, it is possible that I may end by really becoming incapable of doing it. On the contrary, if I shall have the belief that I can do it, I shall surely acquire the capacity to do it, even if I may not have it at the beginning.

—*Mahatma Gandhi*

can't do something, then your actions growing up are probably consistent with that belief. If you try something over and over again, but don't succeed, it's easy to fall into the trap of thinking you'll never succeed. So you stop trying.

Don't Stop Believing

To be fair, it's important to realize that you won't achieve *every* goal you set. Adversity is an important part of life, and you will learn valuable lessons during those times when you fall short of your aspirations.

But you should never allow adversity to cause you to stop believing. Don't be like the elephants described above, which are limited by an imaginary constraint. Instead, bust out of the restraints of your own limited thinking.

> *Once you have decided what you want, act as if it were impossible to fail, and it shall be!*
>
> —Dorothea Brande

Whether you think you *can* accomplish your goals and aspirations, or you think you *can't* achieve your goals, you are right. Develop the confidence to do whatever you set your mind to. Know that you can accomplish great things.

And you will.

It was the last day of the semester, and students filed into the classroom to take the final exam. It had been a tough semester, and the students had all worked very hard. The professor entered, and walked to the lectern at the front of the room.

"I've decided not to require a final exam," he said, much to the delight of the students. "You may leave now, and I'll give you a B for the semester."

About two-thirds of the students opted for the B. They quickly exited the room, chatting and smiling about the "easy B" they had just received.

Before long, only 14 of the original 47 students remained in the room. As the professor passed out the exam to the remaining students, he told them to read it thoroughly, and follow the instructions. When the exam was placed on each student's desk, it read:

Congratulations, you have just received an "A."

Always believe in yourself!

LIFE LESSONS

✓ One of the most powerful keys to success is a belief in your ability to accomplish whatever you set your mind to. Take a few minutes each day, and think about your goals in life. What beliefs must you have in order to achieve those goals?

✓ Continue to take actions to bolster your belief. For example, if one of your goals is to play college soccer, you must believe in your ability to make the team. In order to reinforce that belief, attend a soccer camp, work out with a trainer, or simply increase the amount of time you spend on the soccer field. Resolve to be the best you can be!

Thinking

If you think you are beaten, you are.
If you think you dare not, you don't.
If you'd like to win but you think you can't,
It's almost a cinch you won't.

If you think you'll lose, you're lost,
For out of the world we find
Success begins with a fellow's will—
It's all in the state of mind.

If you think you're outclassed, you are;
You've got to think high to rise;
You've got to be sure of yourself before
You can ever win a prize.

Life's battle doesn't always go
To stronger or faster men;
But sooner or later the man who wins,
Is the one who thinks he can.

Walter D. Wintle

**"No matter how intense things get, you manage
to keep a cool head. What's your secret?"**

CHAPTER 3

Develop A Winning Attitude

The longer I live, the more I realize the impact of attitude on life. Attitude, to me, is more important than facts. It is more important than the past, than education, than money, than circumstances, than failures, than successes, than what other people think or say or do. It is more important than appearances, giftedness, or skill. It will make or break a company, a home. The remarkable thing is we have a choice every day regarding the attitude we will embrace for that day. We cannot change our past. We cannot change the fact that people will act in a certain way. We cannot change the inevitable. The only thing we can do is play on the one string we have, and that is our attitude. I am convinced that life is 10% of what happens to me and 90% how I react to it. And so it is with you—we are in charge of our attitudes.

—Charles Swindoll

Temporary Setbacks

Entrepreneur and inventor Thomas Edison told anyone who would listen that it would take just a couple of weeks for him to invent the light bulb. He gathered the materials he thought he needed and, as the world watched, attempted to introduce the much-anticipated electric light.

But the job wasn't as easy as Edison thought it would be. He knew carbon filaments were one key to a successful light bulb. But when all was said and done, he couldn't find a carbonized plant fiber that would do the trick. After thousands of plant fibers that didn't work, after thousands of prototypes, after thousands of failed attempts, Edison finally illuminated the room—and the world—with the electric light bulb.

How long did this take? Well, not the two weeks he anticipated. Not even two months. When all was said and done, it took Edison two *years* to invent the light bulb.

Most people in Edison's shoes would have given up long before the two-year point. What kept him going? His *attitude*. Edison viewed failures as temporary setbacks that were an integral process of success. When asked how he was able to persevere despite thousands of failures, he said, "I have not failed. I've just found 10,000 ways that won't work."

ATTITUDE IS ALTITUDE

Nick Vujicic was born in Melbourne, Australia, in 1982. Despite his mother having an uneventful pregnancy, and despite the fact there was no family history of genetic abnormalities, Nick was unexplainably born into this world with no arms and no legs.

Think about that for a second. No arms and no legs. His parents couldn't help but wonder how Nick would live a happy, productive life without the ability to hold someone's hand, hug someone, walk, run, or even stand up.

As a young child Nick dealt with the depression, loneliness, and self-esteem issues that all children deal with, but his were magnified by his differences. Gradually, though, Nick began to adapt. He found he was able to accomplish tasks that you would assume required limbs—brushing his teeth, combing his hair, using a computer, and participating in sports. By the time he was in 7th grade not only had Nick accepted his situation, he embraced it and all of the challenges that went with it.

Nick attended college, and earned bachelor's degrees in both accounting and financial planning. He decided that his life's purpose was to inspire and motivate others. At the age of 19, he began telling his story at seminars, at schools, in crowded auditoriums, places of work, and in prisons. Soon, Nick was traveling the world as a sought-after motivational speaker. In 2005 Nick was nominated for the "Young Australian of the Year" award. By the time he turned 27 years old, Nick had spoken in more than 50 countries, to more than two million people.

When Nick speaks, his goal is to share the importance of vision, dreaming big, and of examining perspective and looking beyond your circumstances. He encourages others to view obstacles as opportunities to grow, rather than as problems.

Nick says, "Attitude is Everything, and Self Perception Determines Direction."

AN ETERNAL OPTIMIST

Eight-year-old Cindy was an eternal optimist, and always looked on the bright side of every situation. Her brother, Tommy, was just the opposite. Tommy managed to find fault with just about everything, and he resented his younger sister's happiness. He often teased his younger sister, probably to make himself feel better.

Cindy's favorite holiday was Christmas. Each year she would help decorate the house, and Cindy and her mom would bake cookies together. Tommy always refused to participate in the festivities, and attempted to ruin the mood with his cynical, Scrooge-like comments.

One year, Tommy decided to do something once and for all to extinguish Cindy's Christmas spirit. In the ultimate gesture of meanness, Tommy decided he would give Cindy a box of horse manure. He was tired of "Little Miss Perfect's" positive attitude, and would teach her an important lesson about life.

Christmas morning came, and Tommy couldn't wait to see the look on his sister's face when she opened her present. Tommy grinned as he handed Cindy the box, thinking about how quickly Cindy's disposition would change when she saw her gift.

Cindy quickly removed the wrapping paper, opened the box, and was greeted by both the sight and smell of Tommy's present. "Yippee," she exclaimed, much to the chagrin of her brother. "Where's the pony?"

Attitude is a Choice

We all have the opportunity to choose how we will approach life. You can *choose* to approach life with a positive attitude. You can *choose* to find the positive lessons in the obstacles and challenges that life sometimes throws at you. You can *choose*, as Winston Churchill said, "to see the opportunity in every difficulty." And those choices will make all the difference in your life.

Just how important is attitude? A study by Harvard University revealed that 85% of our success is determined by our attitude, and only 15% because of our technical expertise. John Maxwell writes about this in his book, *Talent is Never Enough*. You can have all the talent and opportunity in the world yet never achieve the success you desire.

> *Nothing can stop the man with the right mental attitude . . . nothing on earth can help the man with the wrong mental attitude.*
>
> —*Thomas Jefferson*

Attitudes do make the difference. Professor Erwin Schell, former Dean of the MIT Department of Business and Engineering, writes, "When our attitude is right, our abilities reach a maximum of effectiveness, and good results inevitably follow." We see this time and time again. Salespeople with the right attitudes outperform their "attitude-challenged" colleagues. Students with great attitudes get good grades, and enjoy the educational process. Right attitudes make all the difference when dealing with people, including our spouses, children, parents, friends, and co-workers. Attitudes help us win in every situation in life.

The following story provides a great illustration about attitude:

> A woman approached three bricklayers, and asked them what they were doing. "Laying bricks," the first bricklayer answered. The

second replied, "Making $17.50 an hour." The third bricklayer said, "Me? I'm building the world's greatest cathedral!"

Each of us has a choice. Like the bricklayers, you are given the opportunity to choose how you will approach life. Attitude is a gift that you can give yourself. Choose, starting today, to have a positive attitude.

> *"It is our choices, Harry, that show what we truly are, far more than our abilities."*
>
> —*Professor Albus Dumbledore, in* Harry Potter and the Chamber of Secrets

Stuff Happens

You can't get through life without bad stuff happening. You just can't. When you consider some of the bad stuff that happens to people—job lay-offs, health issues—it's clear that they are often well beyond our control. However, what you *can* control is how you react to these situations. Essentially, you have two choices: you can choose to focus on the problem, or you can choose to focus on the solution.

People who focus on the problem tend to spend an inordinate amount of time complaining about their "bad luck," or blaming others for their problems. People who are solution-oriented, on the other hand, focus on "fixing" problems. Instead of blaming their situation on bad luck or other people, they take responsibility for improving their situation. Remember what Charles Swindoll said—life is 10% what happens to you, and 90% how you react to it.

> *The one thing you can't take away from me is the way I choose to respond to what you do to me. The last of one's freedoms is to choose one's attitude in any circumstance.*
>
> —*Viktor Frankl*

Is it possible to maintain a positive attitude 100% of the time? Of course not. There will always be situations that will get you down. But like other areas of your life, you can continually work on—and improve—your attitude.

Any time something bad happens to you, think of being given a bag of cement and a bucket of water. What can you do with these two items? You can either build a stumbling block, or you can build a stepping stone to wherever you want to go.

Improving Your Attitude

Commit today to developing a winning attitude. Here are some ideas to get you started:

- **Lift yourself up.** Every morning when you wake up, you have a choice about how you are going to approach your day. You can reluctantly open your eyes, and mutter, "Oh geez, what a day this is going to be." Or you rise up and exclaim, "This is the day the Lord has made, and it's going to be a great day!" The choice is yours as to how you will begin each day.

Accept complete responsibility for your actions, and for your life. Stop blaming other people, or circumstances, for your situation. Instead of focusing on the negative, notice the good in everything. Be a "glass is half-full" person. If you're not happy with your situation, then change it. Don't complain if you aren't doing something to change it.

> *The greatest discovery of my generation is that human beings can alter their lives by altering their attitude.*
> —William James

Use positive language, with yourself and with others. Celebrate your accomplishments, because you've worked hard to achieve them. And have fun! Laugh as often as you can. Laughter releases endorphins, and makes you feel good.

- **Build others up.** Once you've lifted yourself up, go ahead and spread your positive attitude. Help people whenever you can. Resist the temptation to speak negatively about others. Encourage others to not only do well, but also to be positive. Be kind to others (or, as

> *Let's agree to use all our energy in getting along with each other. Help others with encouraging words; don't drag them down by finding fault.*
> —*Romans 14:9*

my friend Jeff says, "Don't be a jerk."). Praise others as often as possible. Serve others in various capacities, including random acts of kindness. Focus on adding value to other people. Not only will this benefit them, but it will also reinforce your winning attitude.

- **Express appreciation.** While most of us are quick to recognize and praise big accomplishments, the little things are even more important to recognize. Develop a habit of noticing and commenting on appearance, routine tasks that have been completed, ideas and efforts. Thank others, both verbally and in writing. Studies have shown that expressing appreciation leads to happiness, so it's a win-win. Others feel great for receiving your praise, and you feel better for having given it.

- **Be grateful.** If you are reading this, then you are incredibly blessed. Don't believe me? Then go to the nearest hospital, and look at the babies hooked up to tubes in the neonatal intensive care unit. Or visit terminally ill cancer patients on the oncology floor. Read about those around the world who are being persecuted for their religious, political, or other beliefs. Google the word "poverty," and learn about the large population of people in the world who are malnourished. You are very fortunate compared to most people in the world, and it's important to recognize that.

- **Fill your mind with inspiration.** Read something positive every day, as a reminder of how blessed you truly are. If you are a Christian, you can find this inspiration in the Bible. There are many other books that can also have a positive impact. Listen to inspirational music as often as you can. Create affirmations that help you focus on a positive future in a world that seems so drawn to negativity. Each of these habits will have a profound impact on your attitude, and on your life.

> *I can do all things through Christ who strengthens me.*
> —*Philippians 4:13*

You have the power within you to direct the course of your life with your attitude. Although you will not always be able to control what happens in your life, you will have the ability to determine your reaction to these events. Develop a winning attitude—starting today!

Life Lessons

✓ Resolve today that you are going to approach life with a positive attitude. Choose to see the opportunity in every difficulty, and those choices will make all the difference in your life.

✓ Whenever bad stuff happens, focus on the solution, not the problem. Take responsibility for improving your situation, and avoid playing the "blame game."

✓ Take out a sheet of paper, and make a list of everything you can do to develop a winning attitude. How can you lift yourself up? How can you build others up? What can you read daily to fill your mind with inspiration? Whatever your answers are to these questions, take action today.

To learn more about *Life Lessons,* go to:
www.lifelessonsthebook.com

"Remember son, when life hands you lemons, try,
try again because a penny saved gathers no moss.
That pretty much covers everything."

CHAPTER 4

Live A Values-Based Life

Get your core values determined and squared away and they will be your guiding principles for every decision, every project you take on or say "yes" to and every goal you go for.
—Howard Schultz

The Cherry Tree
(adapted from the story by Mason Locke Weems)

When George Washington was about six years old, he received a new hatchet. He was very excited about the hatchet, and before long he was outside chopping everything he could find.

A couple days later, George was wandering through his mother's garden. Swinging his arm freely, he was quite amused as he hacked away at his mother's pea sticks. After frolicking about, George looked up. Directly in front of him was a beautiful, young English cherry tree. Wasting no time, George quickly downed the small tree with his new hatchet.

It turned out that George's father was very fond of that particular tree. When George's father discovered that someone had chopped it down, he was furious. He stormed around, questioning everyone in sight. But no one was able to provide any information.

Some time later, George walked into the house, carrying his little hatchet. His father, seeing the hatchet, asked his son if he knew anything about the cherry tree being chopped down.

George stood in silence for a moment, staring down at the floor. Then, he raised his head, and looked his father straight in the eye. "Father, you know I cannot tell a lie. I chopped down the cherry tree with my new hatchet."

Seeing George's remorseful look, his father's demeanor immediately changed. He walked over to George, and lifted the young boy up into his arms. "Son, I'm disappointed that you cut down the cherry tree. But telling me the truth means more to me than a thousand trees! I'm proud of you for accepting responsibility for your actions, and for telling the truth."

THE GOOD SAMARITAN

A man was going down from Jerusalem to Jericho, when he fell into the hands of robbers. They stripped him of his clothes, beat him and went away, leaving him half dead.

A priest happened to be going down the same road, and when he saw the man, he passed by on the other side. So too, a Levite, when he came to the place and saw him, passed by on the other side.

But a Samaritan, as he traveled, came where the man was; and when he saw him, he took pity on him. He went to him and bandaged his wounds, pouring on oil and wine. Then he put the man on his own donkey, took him to an inn, and took care of him.

The next day he took out two silver coins and gave them to the innkeeper. "Look after him," he said, "and when I return, I will reimburse you for any extra expense you may have."

Luke 10:30–35

A TALE OF TWO WOLVES

One evening an old Cherokee told his grandson about a battle that goes on inside people.

> *The truth of the matter is that you always know the right thing to do. The hard part is doing it.*
>
> —Norman Schwartzkopf

He said, "My child, the two 'wolves' are in constant battle with one another."

"One is Evil. It is anger, envy, jealousy, sorrow, regret, greed, arrogance, self-pity, guilt, resentment, inferiority, lies, false pride, superiority, and ego.

"The other is Good. It is joy, peace, love, hope, serenity, humility, kindness, benevolence, empathy, generosity, truth, compassion, and faith."

The boy pondered his grandfather's explanation, and then asked, "Which wolf wins?"

"That's easy," said the old Cherokee. "The wolf that wins is the one you feed."

Clarifying Your Values

Values are the principles or qualities that are important to us. They represent our highest priorities and our most deeply held beliefs—the things that really matter to each of us. Values act as a kind of "moral compass." Just as a compass helps us find navigational direction, values help us find direction about how to live our lives. Ultimately, values provide clear rules and guidelines for how we behave, and are the driving force behind our actions, deeds, and decisions.

Everyone has values, whether we are consciously aware of them or not. We learn many of our values from our parents, teachers, coaches, religious leaders, and other influential people in our lives. We also learn values from our environment—books we read, television shows we watch, and our exposure to the media.

Our values are also shaped by our own experiences. Each experience, whether positive or negative, provides an opportunity to learn and grow. Over time, these experiences also contribute to the development of our values.

> *It's not hard to make decisions when you know what your values are.*
>
> *—Roy Disney*

Taking the time to develop an awareness of and appreciation for your values is one of the greatest gifts you can give yourself. When you know what your values are—when you are aware of what you believe in and what defines your character—you can choose every day to live those values. Your values will lead you like a compass to the things that are most important to you, and they will also make it easier to say "no" to the things that do not support or serve you. To the extent that you live in alignment with your values, your life will be far more fulfilling.

Having clarity about your values also helps you model values-based living for others. If you are a parent, you have the opportunity to model the values you most want to pass on to your children. If you have younger siblings, you can positively impact their lives to the extent that they see you living in alignment with your values. When you model values-based living, you positively impact other people.

When Goals and Values Are Out of Alignment

Dan is a young man in his late twenties. He and his wife Julie met in college, dated for three years, and then got married the summer after they graduated. They have two beautiful children, and they just celebrated their sixth anniversary.

Throughout his life, Dan has been a goal-setter. He did well academically throughout high school and college. As a high school athlete, he earned varsity letters in both basketball and tennis. His success has continued in his career. Dan has worked very hard to get where he is today, and he has even bigger aspirations for himself and his family.

Although they live in a cute bungalow in a great family neighborhood, Dan and Julie both want to move to someplace bigger. Dan has his eye on a four-bedroom colonial across town. It already has a built-in swimming pool, and a big backyard where the kids can play. He wants to enjoy evenings and weekends with his wife and children in their new home, and to create lifelong memories.

Dan is certainly on track to achieve his financial goals. After finishing his MBA, he became a management consultant with a global consulting and technology services company. He earns more than he expected at this stage of his life, and he and Julie are well positioned to purchase their dream house.

> *Personal leadership is the process of keeping your vision and values before you and aligning your life to be congruent with them.*
>
> —*Stephen Covey*

There's just one challenge in an otherwise great life. As a consultant, Dan has to travel to his Fortune 100 clients, who are all over the country. He typically leaves either Sunday night or early Monday morning, and doesn't return until late Friday. His engagements last several weeks, leaving him little time with his family.

Dan's career is skyrocketing, and he is earning great money. But his schedule is wearing him down. When Dan gets home on Friday, all he wants to do is decompress from his arduous week out of town. His children don't understand why "daddy doesn't want to play," and Dan and Julie are both feeling the strain of Dan's career demands.

This is certainly not what Dan had in mind when he set goals around his career and family life. So, what went wrong? After all, Dan worked hard in college to get to where he is today, and his career is exactly where he envisioned it—maybe even better. He should be happy, right?

Life's ups and downs provide windows of opportunity to determine your values and goals.

—Marsha Sinetar

The problem is, Dan's goals are not in alignment with his values. Dan loves his wife and children more than anything in the world, and one of his core values is spending time with his family. However, his career is in direct conflict with that value. Until Dan's work schedule allows him to be home evenings and weekends with his family, he will not be able to experience true happiness.

Building Life Around Your Values

At some point in your life, you have probably thought about your life goals. Maybe you even went through the exercise of writing them down on paper. I strongly encourage you to do so, if you haven't already.

One thing to keep in mind, though, is how those goals line up with your values. If they are not in sync, you can reach your goals, but still fall short of satisfaction and contentment.

It's important to build your life, and your goals, around your values. You can accomplish this by taking the following steps:

1. Identify your values.

Those who have already done a significant amount of work in this area may be aware of their values. Others may have to do some serious soul searching. If you fall into the latter group, begin by asking yourself a few simple questions, such as: What is most important to you in life (family, career, health, your integrity, a relationship with Christ)? What makes you feel good in life (raising a family, climbing the corporate ladder, staying fit physically, helping those less fortunate

> *Finally, brothers, whatever is true, whatever is noble, whatever is right, whatever is pure, whatever is lovely, whatever is admirable— if anything is excellent or praiseworthy—think about such things.*
>
> *—Philippians 4:8*

than you, sharing your faith with others)? What makes you feel valuable (providing for your family, accolades in your business or career, making a certain salary, contributing a certain amount to charities, maintaining great friendships)?

2. Set goals based on your values.

You may be able to achieve your goals, but unless they are aligned with your values, you are not going to be happy. Eventually, your motivation will wear down and you'll have trouble achieving your goals. Begin by taking a look at your values. Are your goals aligned with them? If not, how can you change your goals to better align with your values?

3. Reinvent your life around these values.

Now that you've identified what you need to do, begin to align your life around your values and goals. Set short- and long-term goals to support your values. When you know deep down inside what your values are, and live your life in alignment with those values, you will feel a great sense of purpose and fulfillment. You will be living the life you want to live, and you will feel very good about the person you're becoming.

Live Your Values Every Day

Dan and Julie, the couple from earlier in the chapter, had worked hard to create a great life. But as Dan was climbing the corporate ladder, he forgot to take one key piece into account: his values. Of course, he's not the only person to do so. Many people start their adult lives without contemplating the role values plays in life planning and goal setting. Then they wonder later in life why they don't feel like they are fulfilled. They see greater contentment in their friends and colleagues and wonder, "What are they doing that I'm not?"

> *Try not to become a man of success but rather try to become a man of value.*
>
> —*Albert Einstein*

When it comes to success, resist the temptation to compare yourself with everyone else. We all have different values, and your interpretation of success might be significantly different from that of your friend or colleague. Be wary of trying to live up to other people's expectations, as you might end up living your life according to someone else's values, rather than your own.

Be true to yourself by living a values-based life. Make the decision to live life in alignment with your values, and to orient your goals so they are consistent with those values. As you begin to live in sync with your values, you will feel an incredible sense of fulfillment, contentment, and happiness.

LIFE LESSONS

✓ What is most important in your life? What are the key organizing principles of your life? Take out a sheet of paper, and write down every positive adjective that describes the personality and character you aspire to have. After you complete this exercise, review the Values List in the back of this book to see if any other values apply.

✓ Read through your list of values. If you could orient your life around just five values, which ones would you choose? Circle those values that you feel are most important. These are your core values. Once you have your core values, organize them in order of priority with your most important value being number one, the second most important being number two, and so on.

✓ On another piece of paper, write down the 25 most important goals you want to do, be, and have in your life.

✓ Compare your core values to your goals. Are they congruent? In areas where values and goals clash, reexamine and/or rewrite your goals so they are properly aligned with your values.

You can find free downloadable resources at the *Life Lessons* website:

www.lifelessonsthebook.com

"Cheshire Puss," asked Alice. *"Would you tell me, please, which way I ought to go from here?"*

"That depends a good deal on where you want to go," said the Cat.

"I don't much care where," said Alice.

"Then it doesn't matter which way you go," said the Cat.

— Lewis Carroll, in *Alice's Adventures in Wonderland*

"I'm successful in business because I'm lucky.
But I didn't get lucky until I started working 90 hours a week!"

CHAPTER 5

Strive To Do Your Best

Every morning in Africa a gazelle wakes up. It knows it must run faster than the fastest lion, or it will be killed. Every morning in Africa a lion wakes up. It knows it must outrun the slowest gazelle, or it will starve to death. It doesn't matter whether you are a lion or a gazelle—when the sun comes up, you had better be running.

—Author Unknown

The Best Taxi Driver in Greece

George Kokkotos was a New York restaurant owner who missed his native Greece, and the family and friends he had left behind. After saving money for years, George sold his restaurant, packed up his belongings, and returned to the country he had always called home.

George loved everything about Greece—the azure blue sea, the towns and villages steeped in history, and the people. But making a living was proving to be more difficult than he thought. In order to put food on the table, George resorted to driving a taxi.

> *Do your best every day, and your life will gradually expand into satisfying fullness.*
>
> —Horatio W. Dresser

One day he picked up a travel writer who had just come from a motivational seminar. George confided in the writer how much he loved Greece, but how difficult it was to make a living. The travel writer passed on some important advice he had just learned at the seminar. "If you are going to be a taxi driver," he said, "strive to be the *best* taxi driver." George thought about the writer's advice, and decided to make that his goal.

George replaced his used VW Jetta with a brand new, air-conditioned Mercedes Benz. He began to study the history of Greece, so he could offer information and be more than just a driver. His grasp of the English language enabled him to translate for his clients. Instead of providing the customary silent service associated with so many taxi drivers, George turned every taxi ride into a "tour."

George forged relationships with travel agencies, helping them with transfers from the airport to the hotels, to cruise ships, to ferry boats—anything to make their clients' trips to Greece easier. His highly personalized service was recognized and appreciated by both the travel agencies and their clients.

Before long, George had earned a reputation for offering quality, innovation, and unparalleled service. His business flourished, and he was able to add several more drivers and taxis, including a limousine. Today, many websites, travel guides, and agencies describe George Kokkotos as "The Best Taxi Driver in Greece."

> *Achievement is largely the product of steadily raising one's levels of aspiration and expectation.*
>
> —*Jack Nicklaus*

Those who have the opportunity to engage George's service think of him as much more than just a taxi driver. George likes to tell his clients, "When we say goodbye at the airport, you will be saying goodbye to a friend you will always remember and hope to see again." There have been more than a few tearful goodbyes as his "friends" bid farewell to Greece—and to George.

Gourmet Sandwich Success

Jimmy John Liautaud learned about determination and hard work very early in life. His father was a door-to-door salesman who always worked hard to provide for his family. The lesson of creating security by working harder than anyone else was not lost on Jimmy John. In fact, "work harder than anyone else" became Jimmy John's philosophy.

In the Liautaud family, all the kids were expected to go to college, start a business, or join the Army. Since Jimmy John graduated second to last in his high school class, college certainly wasn't his first choice. In spite of his father's desire, he wasn't overly excited about become "Pvt. Liautaud" either.

> *There is no substitute for hard work.*
>
> —*Thomas A. Edison*

Jimmy John decided to open a Chicago-style hot dog stand. He convinced his father to loan him $25,000 to start the business. His father agreed, with the stipulation that if the venture failed, Jimmy John would enlist in the Army.

In 1983, the ambitious 19-year-old opened his first sandwich shop, near Eastern Illinois University. The 600-square-foot converted garage had formerly housed a pizza business and a donut shop, both of which failed.

The poor location was the least of Jimmy John's challenges. Both friends who had agreed to help him quit within the first few months. In order to survive, Jimmy John worked from 8 a.m. to 3 a.m. for 120 days straight.

Liautaud's determination and hard work helped him survive the early days, and is a huge reason for his continued success. His passion and commitment to excellence is the driving force behind a corporate culture that desires to be the best. It's also a huge factor in the growth of Jimmy John's Gourmet Sandwiches to over 1,000 stores.

Super Bowl MVP

Jerry Rice is one of the best receivers in pro football history. When he retired after 20 seasons, he held 38 NFL records, including regular season receptions (1,549), touchdowns (208), receiving yards (22,985), and consecutive games with at least one reception (274). He has three Super Bowl rings with the San Francisco 49ers, was Super Bowl MVP in 1988, was invited to the Pro Bowl 13 times, and was named to the NFL 75th Anniversary All-Time Team.

Always dream and shoot higher than you know you can do. Don't bother just to be better than your contemporaries or predecessors. Try to be better than yourself.

—William Faulkner

Rice's life began far from the spotlight, however. One of eight children, he grew up in rural Mississippi. His father was a bricklayer, and Jerry and his brothers helped in the summer by tossing and catching bricks. "It taught me the meaning of hard work," Rice said.

That hard-work ethic continued throughout Rice's football career. He worked harder than anyone else in practice, treating practice drills as if they were playoff games. He meticulously studied game films, cataloguing the mannerisms of defensive backs he would face, and also studying the top receivers, to see how they ran their routes and what they did to get open.

Rice's off-season conditioning was unparalleled, and is probably the clearest indication of his determination to be the best. While his con-temporaries were playing golf and enjoying the off-season, Rice continued his relentless quest to perform at a very high level. His strenuous schedule began at 6:00 a.m. every day, and included stretching, speed work, and weight lifting.

> *Nobody who ever gave his best regretted it.*
> —*George Halas*

His years of sacrifice, determination, and hard work solidified Jerry Rice's position as one of the greatest wide receivers of all time.

A Lifelong Promise

When I was in second grade, I became a cub scout. Once a week I walked to my friend Mark's house. Seven other boys and I watched *Speed Racer* until his mother, our den leader, called the meeting to order. We always started with the Cub Scout Promise:

I, (insert first name), promise to do my best
To do my duty to God and my country,
To help other people, and
To obey the Law of the Pack.

Every week, I promised to do my best. And it's a philosophy for living I've embraced ever since.

Does that mean I've always been the best at everything I've ever done? Of course not. No matter how hard I tried—no matter how vehemently I promised to not settle for second best—there were often people who were better than me. I've given my all and come in second—and third, and fourth, and even beyond—enough times to learn that it's really not the reward of being the best that propels me to try my best. It's what I get out of the effort.

Why should you strive to do your best? First, it enables you to live with no regrets. If you've done your best there's no need to ask yourself questions like, "What could I have accomplished if I had tried harder?" You've done your best, and you know

> *We must motivate ourselves to do our very best, and by our example lead others to do their best as well.*
>
> *—S. Truett Cathy*

it. There's no need to wonder or second-guess yourself, and you can feel satisfied with your effort.

In addition, consistently striving to do your best will provide you with unique learning experiences. When you push yourself, you are bound to make mistakes. And when you make mistakes, you learn from them. If you settle for "okay" there's a good chance you'll achieve "okay"—and you won't be able to look back and reflect upon how you could improve in the future. Trying to do your best allows you to accept yourself as you are—while also constantly trying to do better.

It Begins With Hard Work

A relentless commitment to always doing your best is one of the key ingredients of success. In fact, I believe it is the most important controllable ingredient for success. Anyone I have ever met, studied, learned from, or read about who has achieved greatness in any area has done so because of hard work and a strong commitment to being the best they can be. In order to reach your full potential and realize your goals and aspirations, you will need to work hard, too.

> *I'm a great believer in luck, and I find the harder I work, the more I have of it.*
> —*Thomas Jefferson*

It's important to mention that it's not enough to just work hard. Many people work hard, and yet still fall short of their desired level of success. I attribute much of the success I've achieved to luck, and also to being in the right place at the right time. But someone once defined luck as "when preparedness meets opportunity." The preparation part of that equation originates with a commitment to do your best, and a willingness to work very, very hard.

The great business philosopher Jim Rohn used to talk about a simple but powerful concept called *The Ant Philosophy*. The first part of the philosophy is that *ants never quit*. Remember what happened when you put an obstacle in front of where they were walking? They'd look for another way to get where they were going. Ants climb over, or under, or around. No matter what, they never stopped.

Secondly, *ants think winter all summer*. Ants know that summer will not last forever. They gather food all summer, so they're ready for winter. Squirrels do this, too. They gather nuts during the summer, so they're prepared when winter comes. Successful *people* do this, too.

Next, *ants think summer all winter*. Ants know that winter won't last forever, and they're constantly thinking ahead to the summer. When summer hits, they're ready. They hit the ground running.

The last part of Rohn's philosophy answers the question of how much the ant will gather during the summer month's to prepare for winter. The answer? *All it possibly can.* Winters, like economic recessions, job loss, and other adversities, come and go. Those who recognize that, and plan accordingly, will be fine through the winter, or through the storm.

This is a great philosophy, and one I hope you'll live by.

Whatever You Are, Be a Good One

One of the responses I get when I'm talking about the work ethic of successful people is "Well, I'd work hard, too, if I was getting paid millions of dollars a year to _____ (fill in the blank with glamorous job: "play professional football," "be a movie star," tour the world playing my guitar," etc.).

> *No matter what you're doing, try to work at that task like it's your dream job.*
>
> —*Russell Simmons*

The important thing to remember is that people don't start out being Super Bowl MVPs, or Academy Award winning movie stars, or rock stars. For that matter, they don't start out being great parents, or couples who have been happily married for 50 years, either. They start wherever they are.

Consider the early jobs of these now famous celebrities:

• Before he became recognized all over the world as James Bond, Sean Connery was a milkman.

- Before founding Dell Computers, Michael Dell began his working life as a dishwasher in a Chinese restaurant—for less than $3 an hour.
- Before she became one of Hollywood's leading actresses, Julia Roberts worked in an ice cream shop.
- Before he made the world laugh, Jerry Seinfeld sold light bulbs by telephone.
- As a teenager, pop star Madonna worked at a donut shop.

The truth is, it's a rare individual who graduates from school and is instantly catapulted to their dream job. As a matter of fact, most successful people have extremely humble beginnings.

It's easy, when you are flipping burgers or parking cars, to convince yourself that these humble beginnings don't matter. "What's the point of being good at this menial job?" you might ask. "I'll do better when I'm doing something that matters." The fact is, all jobs matter—even

> *Don't be afraid to give your best to what seemingly are small jobs. Every time you conquer one it makes you that much stronger. If you do the little jobs well, the big ones tend to take care of themselves.*
>
> *—Dale Carnegie*

menial, humble jobs. The way you approach those "less-than-dream jobs" will have an effect on your future success.

The Ladder of Success

Think of your career as a ladder. You can't proceed to the next rung if you haven't mastered the first rung. In order to move up to a better paying, more interesting job, you must first master the one you are doing. The thing to remember is that it's not about the job itself. It's about becoming the kind of person you need to be in order to succeed at that job.

Malcolm Gladwell, in his book *Outliers*, answers the question of why successful people are successful in two words—time and commitment. Referring frequently to the "10,000 Hour Rule" created by Florida State University's Dr. K. Anders Ericsson—which states that it takes about 10,000 hours to master any skill—Gladwell shows example after example of real-world success stories that share one thing in common: they work much, *much* harder than anyone else.

- Chess master Bobby Fischer studied chess intensively every day for nine years.
- Bill Gates practiced programming from the time he was in high school, and had open-ended access to some of the country's most sophisticated computers.
- By the time the Beatles "took America by storm" in 1964, they had already performed live over twelve hundred times!

I often remind my children that "the road on the extra mile is never crowded." There is simply no substitute for practice and hard work. You might be talented in a given area, and "luck" certainly enters into the picture, too. But hard work pays off much more significantly than talent or luck. And that's good news for anyone who has ever been told they are lacking "talent" or "natural ability."

If you work hard, you are far more likely to be successful. It's that simple. Anyone who has put in the time and extra effort to achieve a goal knows how true this is. People who stand out in their field will tell you that the extra steps they had to take to get there were difficult—sometimes even painful. But it was worth it, because it elevated them to a level beyond those who were not willing to work as hard.

The late Ohio State football coach Woody Hayes said it best when he said, "I've had smarter people around me all my life, but I haven't run into one yet who can outwork me. And if they can't outwork you, those smarts aren't going to do them much good. That's just the way it is. And if you believe that and live by it, you'd be surprised by how much fun you can have."

Where to Focus Your Excellence

It's difficult to excel at what you do if you don't enjoy what you are doing. There are many people who really dislike their jobs. They dread going to work on Monday, and spend the week thinking about what they are going to do once the weekend rolls around. Then the weekend rolls around, and they dread the fact that Monday is just around the corner. There are more than a few people stuck in this vicious circle. You might even know someone like that.

These people tell themselves that it's okay to do an average job now, because they'll do a bang-up job once they get the promotion—and job—they really want. The problem is, they never get that promotion. Their mediocre performance keeps them out of the running.

Don't be one of those people. Make the decision now—wherever you are in life—that you will not settle for mediocrity. Life is too short to settle for average performance.

> *Your time is limited, so don't waste it living someone else's life. Don't let the noise of others' opinions drown out your own inner voice. And most important, have the courage to follow your heart and intuition.*
>
> —*Steven Jobs*

The first step to being good at what you do is figuring out what you want to do. For example, few people would truly enjoy working the fry machine at a fast food restaurant. But if you love the restaurant industry, and your dream is to eventually own several franchises, suddenly being covered in grease is a lot more palatable. Keep your eye on the prize, and you'll find that doing a good job comes more easily.

Discovering what you want to do with your life is easier said than done. Everyone around you probably has an opinion about what you *should* do with your life. If you find yourself struggling to find your calling, try asking yourself the following questions:

- If you were guaranteed success, what career would you choose?
- If you won the lottery tomorrow and money was no longer an issue, what would you choose to do?
- If you had absolutely no limits, what would be your ideal job?
- What did you love doing as a kid?

> *Whatever you are by nature, keep to it; never desert your line of talent. Be what nature intended you for and you will succeed.*
>
> —*Sydney Smith*

- If you didn't have long to live, what would you want to spend your remaining time on earth doing?
- Where do you want to be in five years?

Once you determine where you want to be, figure out the logical steps it would take to get there. How many rungs are there on the ladder to your dream job?

Understand that not only must you climb each rung, you must also work to be your best at each level. Remember, most people start at the bottom. Those who move up strive to do well at whatever their job is.

> *Success is ... doing what you can do well and doing well whatever you do.*
>
> —Henry Wadsworth Longfellow

Make the commitment now to do your best, in everything you do. Remember the humble beginnings of those who have succeeded before you, and follow in their footsteps. Doing so will not only ensure your success, but you will set an example for those on the rungs beneath you.

Have Fun, Too

While hard work is a key ingredient for success, it can't be the *only* ingredient in your life. Play, fun, sport, and spontaneity are important as well. If you can't step away from working hard on a regular basis—really and truly step away—you'll have a difficult time sustaining the pace.

All too often we forget how to be present. I can't tell you how many times I've been at a sporting event and seen parents exit the auditorium to take a business call on their cell phone. By not being present and fully engaged in our "play" we sacrifice so much. As matter of fact, we often completely miss the wonder of the present.

For me, weekends, holidays, and vacations are great, because they provide a respite from the "hustle and bustle" of my schedule during the week. I have time to think of something other than work, and my wife and children also have a break from their normal activities. It provides an opportunity to be more focused on people, rather than on our schedules.

> *Whatever you do, work at it with all your heart, as working for the Lord, not for men.*
> —Colossians 3:23

It's important to build down time into your life. Commit to being fully present when you "play." Put away the cell phone and shut off the laptop computer. Revel in the moment, as well as in the people you are sharing it with.

Wherever you are, be there.

When cellist Pablo Casals was 93 years old, he was asked why he continued to practice the cello three hours a day. He replied, "I'm beginning to notice some improvement." Casals continued to do his best, even at the age of 93, and even though he was already the undisputed greatest living cellist at the time.

What can we learn from Casals, and others like him? That successful people are committed to excellence, and they never stop striving to do their best.

Life Lessons

✓ Identify the key areas of your life, and write them down. For each area, rank yourself from one to ten. (Ten means you're striving to do your best, and one means you're hardly trying.) What one thing could you do in each area to create better results? Create a plan for improving each area of your life. Strive to do your best in everything you do!

✓ Reread the section on "Where to Focus Your Excellence." Answer the questions in that section. Once you've determined a viable opportunity that will get you where you want to be in five years, write it down on a separate sheet of paper. Review it daily, and do something every day that will move you toward your goal.

✓ Stay focused and committed to doing your best!

"I used to hibernate for four months of the year,
but then a motivational speaker made me realize
this was a form of self-sabotage that was keeping
me from making the most of my potential."

CHAPTER 6

Develop Success Habits, And Practice Them Daily

We are what we repeatedly do. Excellence, then, is not an act, but a habit.

—Aristotle

A Tale of Two Classmates

Ellen and Christine grew up in the same town, and became good friends in high school. Both were excellent students, and when they graduated each received generous scholarships to the state university.

Ellen and Christine continued their friendship throughout college, and were even roommates for two of their four years. Both graduated at the top of their class with majors in English, and then went their separate ways.

Ellen and Christine lost touch with each other for many years, and it wasn't until their 25th college reunion that they were reunited. After greeting each other warmly and getting small talk out of the way, Ellen and Christine were amazed to find that though they lived on opposite coasts, each worked for a division of the same large newspaper conglomerate.

"Then you know how difficult it was to climb the ladder," Ellen said to Christine, rolling her eyes. "Someone was always getting in my way and preventing me from doing what I wanted to do. The promotions I wanted were always given to someone else. Eventually I knew I would be turned down so I didn't even try. I figured I would end up wherever I ended up."

"I know what you mean," commiserated Christine. "Promotions were hard to come by. But I figured if I worked harder than anyone else, I would eventually be rewarded. I decided that I was the one in charge of how far I went in the company, and became intent on finding a solution to ensure that I reached my goals. It certainly wasn't easy, but I never gave up. I had a tremendous amount of self-discipline, never wavered, and always kept my eye on the prize."

"My habits weren't nearly that admirable," Ellen scoffed. "And I don't think it would have made any difference whatsoever if they had been. But I put in my time and I did okay."

"I always knew you would," Christine said. "So what do you do at The Press?"

"I'm a publisher of one of the local papers," Ellen said, puffing out her chest in a manner that clearly said *beat that*. "But I'm curious to know how far your good habits got you. What is it that you do for The Press, Christine?"

"I'm the president and CEO," she said.

RUNNING FROM DEFEAT

The year was 1992, and the setting was the summer Olympics in Barcelona, Spain. British sprinter Derek Redmond was getting ready to race in the 400-meter semifinal. Redmond held the British record in this event, and he was ready to show the world what he could do. This race was all the more important because Redmond had been forced to withdraw from the 400 in the 1988 Games in Seoul, just 10 minutes before the race, because of an Achilles tendon injury.

As 65,000 fans looked on, Redmond broke away from the pack and took the lead. He motored down the backstretch, a mere 175 meters between him and the finals, when suddenly, his hamstring ruptured. Redmond fell to the track helplessly. The pain was so great that Redmond felt like he had been shot. Everything he worked for was finished.

As the rest of the runners crossed the finished line, Redmond stood up. He had trained hard for this particular race, and there was no way he wasn't going to finish it. Redmond hobbled toward the finish, each step more painful than the step before.

With 120 meters left to go, Redmond's father ran onto the track to help his son finish the race. Brushing aside security and track officials, Derek's father Jim put one hand on Derek's forearm, and wrapped his arm around his son. They continued together until they were a couple steps in front of the finish line. Then, Jim released the grip he had on his son, so Derek could finish the race by himself.

Redmond never won the Olympic medal that he wanted, but he became known throughout the world as a "winner" when he crossed that finish line. Instead of accepting defeat, Redmond persevered. He may have come in dead last, but he finished the race. Redmond's finish that day demonstrated to the world what *victory* really means.

Habits Make the Man

He was born from humble beginnings, the son of a snake oil salesman. But when he entered the oil industry at a young age, John D. Rockefeller was determined to be successful by being disciplined in a very undisciplined industry.

While other oil companies were going under as fast as they were cropping up, Rockefeller developed a set of unwavering habits that enabled his company to flourish and dominate. Regardless of the fashions of the day, regardless of what other companies were doing, Rockefeller stayed true to his habits:

- He identified goals and communicated his top priorities quarterly and yearly.
- He developed ways to measure success, and used them regularly.
- He held daily, weekly, monthly, quarterly, and yearly meetings to keep everyone aligned and accountable.

By the age of 30, John D. Rockefeller had created the United States' largest monopoly at the time, Standard Oil, and was considered one of the richest men in the world.

Success is Not an Accident

I am often asked about the characteristics of successful people—the qualities, traits, and habits that make them successful. Those who ask wonder (1) if there are indeed common habits or traits that can be linked to success, and (2) whether they could achieve some level of success by applying those qualities. The answer to both questions is "yes!"

It is important to understand that you are an accumulation of your habits—things you repeatedly do. From what time you get up each morning, what you eat for breakfast, how you dress, the language you use when speaking, how you think, and how you act in the company of others. These things we do—these "habits"—make us who we are.

> *Good habits, once established, are just as hard to break as bad habits.*
>
> *—Robert Puller*

Many people don't realize the impact habits have on our lives. To the extent that you develop good habits, those habits will contribute substantially to your success. For example, you must have good study habits in order to do well academically. You have to eat well to be healthy. In order to be successful in your business or career, you need to develop good work habits. All success is preceded by the development and practice of good habits. Bad habits, on the other hand, can cause you to repeat self-destructive patterns, which will limit your success.

People who are successful plan their success. They continually develop and hone success habits that are in line with the life they want to create. They also drop the bad habits that do not serve them. When you consistently replace your bad habits with good habits, you will become a product of those good habits, and success will soon follow.

Success is not an accident. It is never random. People who are successful aren't merely *lucky*. They aren't successful simply because they were in the right place at the right time. Success rarely rains down upon you. Success is the result of choices you make—as evidenced by your habits—about how you want to live your life. In order to be successful, you must *make* it rain.

Habits of Highly Successful People

What follows is a list of 15 success habits. This is a list I have developed throughout my life. The habits below are not intended to be all-inclusive. But they are all important, if not the *most* important, ingredients for success.

Choose to develop the 15 success habits listed below. Focus on them continually, and integrate them into your daily living. Like a particular skill honed by an athlete, these habits will soon become part of who you are.

Habit #1: Create Clear, Written Goals

In 1953, seniors at Yale University were asked to complete a questionnaire prior to graduation. They were asked the question, "Do you have clear, specific, written goals for your life, and have you developed plans for their accomplishment after you leave the university?"

Of those questioned, 84% had no goals at all, beyond the obvious desire to graduate, leave school, and enjoy the summer. The seniors that had goals, but had not written them down, numbered 13%. Only 3% of the seniors had clear written goals and plans for what they wanted to do when they graduated.

In 1973, twenty years later, members of that class at Yale were surveyed again. One of the questions asked was, "What is your net worth today?"

When the results of the survey were examined, it was discovered that the 3% who had clear, written goals and plans in 1953 had a greater combined net worth than the other 97% put together! Furthermore, clearly written goals and plans was the only characteristic the top 3% had in common. Some had performed well academically, while others had done poorly. Some stayed on the East Coast, while others had moved across the country. The one common trait of the most successful graduates was that they had been intensely goal-oriented.

Highly successful people know where they want to go in life, and they have a clear plan to get there. They are intensely goal-oriented, and their "roadmap to success" is the list of goals that they have written down.

Goal setting is certainly not a new concept. We have all heard about the importance of having goals. For example, we know that Olympic and professional athletes have goals, and constantly strive to achieve them. Amazingly, though, less than 3% of the population have a written set of goals. Furthermore, less than 1% review their goals on a regular basis.

Without goals, people wander around aimlessly, wondering why they have not accomplished their desired results. Goals have been called "dreams with deadlines," and having them will help you to achieve the results you want to create in your life.

There are several reasons to have written goals for your life:

1. Written goals increase your odds of success.

An architect would not think of proposing a building project without a blueprint. Why? Because a blueprint acts as a "roadmap" that helps communicate how the building must be built. Without these plans, the project would be far less efficient, and probably unsuccessful. The same holds true for written goals, as they relate to *your* success.

2. Written goals provide clarity of purpose.

With written goals, and an action plan to support those goals, you will know precisely what you need to do to achieve your desired results. This crystal-clear picture will help you to be more efficient, thereby avoiding the waste of time, money, and effort.

3. Written goals move you steadily toward your goal.

Creating written goals often seems like holding a magnet underneath a sheet of paper filled with iron filings. Like the magnet, your written plan will pull you toward the accomplishment of your goals. This often seems effortless, as if the only action necessary was to write down the goal.

Successful people have clear, written goals. They know exactly who they want to be, where they want to go, and what they want to accomplish. Goal setting is a very powerful technique that can help you to create significant results in every area of your life. Begin today to write down goals for your life!

Habit #2: Take Action . . . Now!

How many great ideas have you had, but not acted upon? Later, you discover that someone else has "taken" your idea, and used it to achieve success. If you're a student, maybe you delayed making a decision about the project you were going to work on, and another student "took" the same idea. If you're an adult, maybe you had a great business idea, then saw your idea show up months later in the marketplace.

Procrastination is one of the biggest challenges we face in our busy lives. Although we really want or need to do something now, we don't do it. Whether it's not taking action on a great new business idea, putting off an undesirable task at work, or

Being maniacal about something is very helpful.
—*Bill Gates*

delaying the inevitable chore at home, procrastination is one of the major stumbling blocks that stand in the way of our success.

Successful people are intensely action-oriented, and you can be, too. Here are several ideas to help you get started:

- **Make a to-do list.** Put everything that needs to be accomplished, large and small, on your list.
- **Set deadlines.** Knowing that we need to accomplish something by a specific time leads us to action.
- **Break tasks into small pieces.** Reducing the task to smaller, more manageable pieces helps to avoid confusion and overwhelm, which are two common causes of procrastination.
- **Commit to just five minutes.** If you make a firm commitment to this short period of time, you will often

continue beyond the initial time. If it's just not happening after five minutes, then stop—at least you got something accomplished.

- **Enlist a buddy.** Making a commitment to another person provides additional support. Make sure the person cares enough to hold you accountable.
- **Take a break.** If you're stuck, take a break for a few minutes. Just make sure you go back after a short break.
- **Do the unpleasant task first.** By getting the hard stuff out of the way first, the rest seems easy (and more doable) by comparison.
- **Build momentum with an easy task.** Sometimes, though, the hard stuff seems too difficult. If that's the case, then start with something easier, but still relevant.

Action-orientation is a critical component of success. Cultivate the habit of doing things now. Not only will you get things done, you'll get things done sooner. Remember, just do *something*, and do it now!

Habit #3: Practice Discipline

Sports radio talk show host Jim Rome was interviewing Kobe Bryant, and they reminisced about a time when they ran into each other in southern California. They drank a beer together, and then Jim had to leave because of a dinner reservation.

"Would you like to join us for dinner?" asked Rome.

"I'd love to," replied Bryant, "but I have to go lift (weights)."

Bryant's response, especially coming from one of the greatest basketball players of all time, didn't surprise Rome. What surprised him was the timing of his response: It was Saturday night at 9:15, in the off-season.

Kobe Bryant would not miss one day of working out, even if it meant putting more enjoyable activities aside. It took Mozart years of daily rigorous practice before he composed his best symphonies. J.K. Rowling knew she wanted to be a writer from the time she was six years old—and since then has set aside time to write every day.

Successful people decide what it's going to take to be successful, and then they do those things. They focus like a laser on their goal, and discipline themselves to follow their plan for achieving that goal. This discipline is not limited to a particular season, or for a specific project. Rather, it is a way of life for all who consistently perform at a high level.

Habit #4: Accept Responsibility

When people are unhappy with their lives, the blame for their unhappiness is often directed outward. If they don't blame it on someone else, then they attribute their misfortune to "bad luck" or "the economy" or how "unfair" the world (or life) is. They seem to blame everything but their own decisions and actions.

This kind of attitude is self-defeating, and stands in the way of possible solutions. If the same amount of energy were directed toward results, it would be very interesting to see the outcome.

Successful people don't make excuses. They don't blame others. They don't whine and complain. They realize that it doesn't matter whose fault anything is. What matters is what they're going to do about it. Successful people accept responsibility for their actions, their circumstances, and their lives. Instead of thinking "My life would be better if . . . ," they think about what they want their lives to look like, and how to make that happen.

Ultimately, you and you alone are responsible for your success. For life to work the way you want it to, you have to work. Take 100% responsibility for your life.

Habit #5: Persistence

It was the late 1840s. After hearing of the gold rush in California, two brothers from Nebraska decided to sell everything they had and move west to stake their claim. They took the Overland Route across the United States, and soon arrived in northern California.

Within the first few days, they had already discovered pieces of the shiny metal along the bank of a river near Sacramento. The men staked their claim to the land, invested in additional prospecting supplies, and continued their quest to make a quick fortune.

Their good fortune continued for the next couple weeks, and then something strange happened. The gold seemed to have disappeared. The two brothers searched and searched, but to no avail. Finally, they gave up, sold their equipment and claim rights for a pittance, and returned back home to Nebraska.

The man who bought the claim didn't know much about prospecting for gold, so he hired an engineer to examine the land. After surveying the property, the engineer advised him to continue digging in the exact spot where the former owners had left off. The man followed the engineer's recommendation, and dug deeper in the same area. Within days, the new owner discovered the "mother lode," and became one of the wealthiest prospectors of the Gold Rush.

Most people give up long before they should. They try something a couple times, and then they stop. Had the two brothers stuck it out longer, they would have become millionaires. Because they gave up prematurely, they arrived back home in Nebraska with less than they had when they left.

The biggest difference between those who succeed and those who don't is not usually talent, but persistence. Highly successful people don't quit. They might feel like it. They might be tempted. But they don't quit.

> *It's not whether you get knocked down; it's whether you get up.*
> —*Vince Lombardi*

Successful people see their vision through to completion no matter how long it takes or how difficult it is.

You'll run into adversity on the road to your goals. It will be easy to quit, and hard to stay the course. When things get tough remind yourself that they are supposed to. Put your head down, plow ahead, and in the words of Winston Churchill, "Never, never, never, never give up."

Habit #6: Enthusiasm

Orville and Wilbur Wright's interest in flying was first created by their father, who gave the boys a small helicopter-like toy made of sticks and paper. The fascination with "things that fly" continued during their childhood when they, along with their friends, flew kites. Wilbur Wright said later that their parents encouraged them "to follow their interests and to investigate whatever aroused their curiosity."

Years later, in the back of their bicycle shop in Dayton, Ohio, the Wright brothers began the pursuit of an interest that had been on their minds for a long time: the construction of a flying machine.

It took three years from the time Wilbur built his first glider until the world's first airplane would leave the ground. After the initial tests of the glider at a remote sandy area four miles south of Kitty Hawk, North Carolina, the Wright brothers constructed a wind tunnel back at their bicycle shop in Dayton. Once they perfected the glider, they developed a propeller, then an engine, for their flying machine. They built the 1903 Flyer in sections, shipped the sections down to Kitty Hawk, and assembled it.

On December 14, 1903, the Wright brothers were ready to fly their machine. They flipped a coin to see who would go first, and Wilbur won the coin toss. In his first attempt, he stalled it and crashed into the sand, causing minor damage. The crash forced them to wait three days, until the repairs were made and the weather conditions were right.

On December 17, Orville made the next attempt. At 10:35 a.m., the flying machine lifted off the ground. It stayed in the air for 12 seconds, and covered just 120 feet. But in that flight, Orville accomplished what people for centuries had only dreamed of . . . he flew.

Successful people are extremely enthusiastic about what they do. In fact, this passion is the fuel that drives them to do what they do. And achievement toward their dream feeds the enthusiasm even more. Imagine the great excitement that Orville and Wilbur Wright must have felt during that first flight at Kitty Hawk!

> *Enthusiasm is one of the most powerful engines of success. Nothing great was ever achieved without it.*
>
> —*Ralph Waldo Emerson*

Enthusiasm will not only inspire your own confidence and drive you, but it will have a positive effect on others, as well. Enthusiasm is contagious. Others will feel your enthusiasm by the way you talk, and the way you act. Henry Ford once said, "Enthusiasm is the yeast that makes your hopes shine to the stars. Enthusiasm is the sparkle in your eyes, the swing in your gait. The grip of your hand, the irresistible surge of will and energy to execute your ideas."

Just as it was for the Wright brothers, Henry Ford, and many others throughout history, let enthusiasm be the yeast that makes *your* hopes shine to the stars. Whatever you are interested in, let your enthusiasm drive you to do that thing in an excellent fashion. Share your enthusiasm with others, too, in a way that will inspire them to achieve greatness. When you live your life with enthusiasm, you will bring out the best in others . . . and in yourself!

Habit #7: Sense of Purpose

All great accomplishment in history occurred because someone had a vision for that achievement. Alexander Graham Bell was fascinated with acoustics and voice patterns, which developed into the invention of the modern telephone. Johannes Gutenberg visualized the spread of literacy to a wider cross section of society, which led to the invention of the mechanical printing press. Thomas Edison, the most prolific inventor in history, devoted his entire adulthood to creating many of today's modern conveniences—the phonograph, incandescent light bulb, motion picture camera and projector, and hundreds more.

Sadly, most people go through life without such a vision. Without this sense of purpose, it is easy to simply go through the motions of life. That's not a bad thing, in and of itself. But when they wonder why life has fallen short of expectations, this is the first area to examine.

Think about it this way: If you are traveling someplace, and you know where you are going, it's much easier to get there. If, on the other hand, you don't know where you are going, how can you expect to get there?

A sense of purpose gives successful people the "reason why" they want to get where they are going. It is the starting point of all achievement. Dr. Napoleon Hill calls this *definiteness of purpose*. In his book, *The Law of Success*, Hill writes about the power of this habit, asserting that "any dominating idea, plan or purpose, held in the mind through repetition of thought and emotionalized with a burning desire for its realization is taken over by the subconscious mind and acted upon through whatever natural and logical means available." In other words, when your sense of purpose is strong enough, your subconscious mind will help you achieve your desired outcome.

Successful people know what they want, and have a burning desire to possess it. They are laser-focused on the achievement of their goals. A sense of purpose brings clarity about the direction of their lives, and moves them much faster toward the accomplishment of their goals.

Your sense of purpose doesn't have to be so big that it will change the world. For a man who just survived a heart attack, he suddenly has a huge "reason why" he needs to live a healthy lifestyle. Parents have a built-in sense of purpose related to their children. High school and college students are at the point in their lives where they have a short-term sense of purpose, and must begin to think about their goals and aspirations after graduation.

Don't rule out the opportunities to change the world, either. Those who have done so didn't start out with the plan of "becoming well-known." They started out with the desire to positively impact a part of humanity that wasn't working. Following are two examples of people who developed a very clear sense of purpose.

Blake Mycoskie, while vacationing in Argentina, was disturbed to discover the number of children there who had no shoes to protect their feet. After doing a bit of research, he learned that many children in developing countries grow up barefoot, which puts them at risk of (1) catching soil-transmitted diseases, (2) getting cuts and sores, which can become infected, and (3) not getting an education, because they are not allowed to attend school without shoes. Mycoskie created TOMS Shoes, which was founded on a simple premise: With every pair of shoes purchased, TOMS will give a pair of new shoes to a child in need. As of April 2010, TOMS has given more than 600,000 pairs of shoes to children around the world.

Jessica Flannery saw an opportunity to deliver financial services to poor people in developing countries. She and her husband, Matt, started an organization called Kiva, whose mission is "to connect people, through lending, for the sake of alleviating poverty." By connecting individuals with money to lend to an entrepreneur across the globe, Kiva has created relationships beyond financial transactions, and built a global community expressing support and encouragement of one another. As of August 2010, Kiva has facilitated more than $150 million in loans.

It's okay if your sense of purpose isn't yet clear. Blake Mycoskie's became clear during a vacation in Argentina. Yours might become clear after reading an article in a magazine, or attending a conference, or through a discussion with a friend.

It might end up being the focus of your life and career, or simply a part of your life. Either way, you'll recognize it, and having the strong sense of purpose will motivate you to achieve yours goals, and to take action toward the accomplishment of those goals.

Habit #8: Adaptability

Today, we are fortunate to be living in the greatest period in human history. There are more opportunities than ever before, and this trend will definitely continue. The world is also changing faster than ever before.

Think about the industries that didn't exist 100 years ago. Automotive, aviation, music recording, health care. Those industries were all born within the last 100 years. Now think about the products that were developed just within the last 30 years. Cell phones, express package delivery (Fed-Ex was not the immediate successor to the Pony Express . . . it came a few years after that), home videos, 24-hour news coverage (which started with CNN and BBC World News), personal computers, the Internet, and biotechnology.

The world is evolving at an accelerating rate. Think about the last five years. YouTube, Twitter, Facebook. By the time you read this book, there will likely be new social networking websites, new technologies, and new products. Try fast forwarding 20 years. How many industries, products, and jobs will be created? How many will be brand new—things we've never even thought of before?

With all the changes going on in the world today, the ability to adapt and remain flexible is no longer optional—it's imperative. Whereas the ability to adapt used to be a choice, it is now an essential ingredient for success.

Charles Darwin said, "It is not the strongest of the species that survive, nor the most intelligent, but the one most responsive to change." His words have never been more true than they are today. So much so, that I believe adaptability is the key success trait of the 21st century.

There are two essential ingredients to becoming more adaptable—embracing change, and being proactive.

1. Embrace change.

When people are faced with change, they react one of two ways. Either they are change-averse, and sometimes even overcome with emotion at the mere prospect of change, or they look forward with eager anticipation to the positive impact the changes will have. Successful people recognize that, like it or not, change is inevitable, and the one thing that can be controlled is their reaction to the change. Think positively about the future, and realize that change is both a challenge and an opportunity.

2. Be proactive.

Successful people always look forward, proactively gathering information about pending changes. Rather than waiting for change, they are often the change agents. They see the opportunities for improvement, whether it is in themselves, in others, in their own organizations, or in the world. By positioning themselves accordingly, they are able to react earlier—and better—than others.

By embracing the ever-changing world in which we live, and developing your ability to adapt to those changes, you will be well positioned to create success in your life.

Habit #9: Optimism

There are two kinds of people in the world: People who think the proverbial "glass" is half-empty, and those who believe it is half full. Successful people are invariably optimistic—they believe the glass is half full. They are optimistic about the future, and they're optimistic about their role in that future.

Below are a few traits of optimists:

- They think about where they're going, and how they will get there (rather than focusing on all the things that could prevent them from getting where they want to go).

- They look for the good in people and in situations (as opposed to finding fault with people and being cynical about situations).
- They see difficulty and temporary setbacks as learning opportunities (rather than getting discouraged and quitting).
- They realize that life is an incredible blessing, and live their lives accordingly (instead of complaining, and/or blaming others for what they don't have).
- They truly expect success, both of themselves and of others. So much so, in fact, that they are enthusiastic about sharing their success with others, and thereby helping them to be successful.

There are tremendous advantages when you view life through the lens of optimism. First, you feel better. You are in a better mood, and you exude positive energy. Secondly, numerous studies have linked optimism to good health. Optimism clearly contributes to living a longer and more prosperous life.

Perpetual optimism is a force multiplier.
—Colin Powell

If you are already an optimist, then continue to believe in yourself and spread your positive energy to those around you. If you find yourself looking at a half-empty glass, then think about ways you can improve in the areas listed above. What causes you to react a certain way, and what could you do to change your reaction? Finally, surround yourself with optimists, because optimism is contagious!

Habit #10: Integrity

Three college students were taking a chemistry class together one semester. They were bright students, and all three had a solid "A" going into the final exam. The Saturday before finals, they went to another school to party with some friends. They didn't make it back to school until early Monday morning. None of the three was in any shape to take the final.

The three students went to their professor's office a half hour before the exam. They explained that they had been out of town, and planned to be back the next day. But they had a flat tire on the way back and didn't have a spare, so they didn't get back to school until that morning.

The professor was a reasonable man, and the three young men were good students. He agreed to let them make up the final the next day. "What a relief!" they thought. The three took showers, grabbed a bite to eat, and then studied the rest of the day and most of that night.

When they arrived for the exam, their instructor placed them in separate rooms, and gave each student the exam. They turned to the first question, worth five points, and all three quickly answered it. Then they turned to the next question, worth 95 points: "Which tire?"

Integrity is the foundation of character, and the single most important habit for success. It is the core habit of a successful and happy life. Unlike the other habits, lacking in this trait is a formula for disaster. By making the commitment to living a life of high integrity, you will do more to ensure your success and happiness than anything else you could do.

> *Always do right. This will gratify some people, and astonish the rest.*
>
> —Mark Twain

When you live a life of integrity, you are committed to honesty, both with others and with yourself. You keep your word. You follow through on what you say you're going to do. By living your life in this manner, you build credibility with those around you. You become known as the kind of person who is trustworthy. You become known for your strong moral character.

Not only is integrity a moral issue, it's a practical one as well. A high standard of personal ethics is crucial for business and personal success. In a joint study conducted by the UCLA Graduate School of Management and Korn/Ferry International of New York, 71% of the executives surveyed said that integrity was the quality most needed to succeed in business.

In spite of this research, there is a growing belief in the world today that people can lack moral character, and yet still be successful. My response to this is that, while they may reach some milestone of accomplishment, they are not "successful people." True success, in my opinion, cannot be achieved without integrity. Sooner or later, the person who lacks integrity will suffer for it.

Habit #11: Courage

At a major teaching hospital in the Midwest, a new nurse manager was starting her first shift. She was in charge of the operating room nursing team, with full responsibility for the duties of the OR nurses.

The surgery was a routine appendectomy, and everything was going fine. The surgeon finished removing the appendix, then said, "Okay, let's close the incision. Sutures, please." The new nurse had followed the surgery very closely, and noticed a problem. "Doctor," she responded, "you used eleven sponges, but only ten have been removed."

The surgeon was taken aback by the new nurse's audacity in questioning him. "I got them all, nurse. Let's get this incision closed." The nurse second-guessed herself for a split second. But she *knew* that one sponge was still inside the patient. "Doctor, think of the patient. You still have another sponge to remove!"

The surgeon looked up at the nurse, paused for a moment, and grinned. "You passed the test, Ms. Jones. You're going to make a fine nurse manager." He removed the eleventh sponge, and then completed the surgery.

It took a lot of courage for the nurse to question the surgeon. It's not always easy to be courageous, but it's one of the qualities of highly successful people. Develop the courage to stand up for what you believe in, and to do the right thing, even when it's not popular.

When you make the decision to stand up for what you think is right, it's important to have your information in order. Also, you must be ready to defend your position. Finally, it's important to know what the consequences may be. The nurse was taking a risk by questioning the doctor, but she knew she was doing the right thing.

Habit #12: Confidence

Successful people believe in themselves, and in their ability to succeed at whatever they do. This confidence removes the limitations created by doubt and fear. When you believe in yourself, and in your abilities, your mind will help you find ways to accomplish your goals.

Confidence is developed over time, as you develop your areas of strength. As you learn and grow, you will recognize that you are strong in certain areas, and not as strong in others. Focus your thoughts on what you do well, and that will help you develop confidence.

An example of this early in life is riding a bike. For most people, this is a difficult task at first. Then, in time, they are able to ride without assistance, and without training wheels. Soon, most people feel extremely confident in their ability to pick up a bike, jump on, and ride it down the street.

> *A mind troubled by doubt cannot focus on the course to victory.*
> —Arthur Golden

Those same dynamics apply to developing confidence in every area of life. Feeling a bit uncertain at first, but continuing to focus on improvement. Visualizing success, and practicing over and over until a certain level of proficiency is attained. Thinking positive thoughts, and disregarding what others might think as you're developing your skill.

Be persistent in your efforts to build confidence in every area of your life. Believe in yourself, and continually back up that belief with concrete evidence of your abilities. You can do it!

Etiquette Habits

The final three habits are a bit different than the previous twelve. I call these "etiquette" habits—practical tips that are critically important to success in the world today.

Two comments about these habits:

1. They are immediately visible to other people.
2. They provide a way for you to quickly differentiate yourself from everyone else.

First impressions are not everything, but they *are* very important. By developing and using these habits consistently, you will make a favorable impression on people you meet and connect with. And quite often, you will set yourself apart from everyone else by practicing these habits.

Habit #13: Arrive Early

Imagine that you have a date with someone special, and she arrives 15 minutes late. How did your excitement about getting together change during those 15 minutes? What if this was the third time in a row this has happened? What if she is *always* 15 minutes late?

Now imagine you are interviewing a candidate for an important position you are trying to fill. The candidate's resume is stellar, and you can't wait to speak with him. The appointed time arrives, but your prospect is nowhere to be found. Forty-five minutes later, he arrives. He seems a bit frazzled, but doesn't apologize for being late. In fact, he doesn't even mention it. How excited are you *now* about hiring him?

In today's busy world, the concept of "fashionably late" has been extended beyond parties to just about every place we have to be at a specific time. Tardiness in schools and the workplace is rampant as we struggle to fit more and more into our lives. Medical offices and hair salons run perpetually behind, as patients and clients arrive late throughout the day.

Ultimately, tardiness is a sign of disrespect. It means you don't value the other person's time. In the case of an interview, it can also suggest you're disorganized or incompetent. Or, it might indicate that you possess other negative qualities, and tardiness is just one manifestation of those qualities.

Either way, it's not good. Being late often goes unnoticed in the short run. Over time, however, your actions develop into a habit. Once it becomes a habit, it's hard to be on time for anything, including "important" events like a job interview.

If you're on time, you're *late*, so make the decision now to be a person who arrives early. This sends a message of commitment and respect for others. Plan your schedule so you arrive a few minutes early for everything. Take some reading material or other activity, in case you arrive earlier than expected and you need to wait for a few minutes. Better for *you* to wait than to keep someone else waiting!

Habit #14: Develop a Million-Dollar Handshake

We've all met someone who has a "bad" handshake. A handshake that is too limp (the "wet noodle"), or too firm (the "bone crusher"). Research and etiquette books both indicate that this initial impression often sets the tone for the entire relationship.

A handshake says a lot about who you are. A firm handshake will help you make a good first impression, whether you are male or female. Make sure your handshake sends the right message. Make sure it is a "million-dollar" handshake.

A million-dollar handshake is relatively simple. It is firm and personable, conveying a friendly attitude. Extend your arm, and grab the other person's hand firmly. Maintain eye contact and smile. Pump your hand up and down twice. That's it!

Habit #15: Send Handwritten Thank You Notes

It's one of the easiest and most powerful things you can do for another person. And yet so many people don't do it. Express your appreciation by sending handwritten thank you notes.

In today's busy, fast-paced society, handwritten communication has become a thing of the past. We are less likely to follow up with a "thank you" at all, and if we do it often arrives in a quick email sent from our iPhone.

When you send a handwritten note, your recipient will appreciate the kind gesture. It will also set you apart from everyone else because, unfortunately, almost no one writes handwritten notes anymore.

Imagine this scenario. You have just finished a job interview. You sit in your car in the parking lot, and write out a heart-felt note of appreciation for the opportunity you just discussed. Because you have a pre-stamped envelope, you mail the thank you note at the nearest post office. It arrives on the desk of your interviewer the next day.

Here's another example. You attend an event, where someone you've been wanting to meet is also in attendance. You are one of many people he will meet that day. That evening, you send a handwritten note saying how great it was to meet him, and how you look forward to seeing him again.

How many people took five minutes out of their day to do what you did? Probably just you. What effect do you think that will have the next time you contact or see that person? Instead of being just another person he met that day, he will never forget "the person who sent the handwritten note."

LIFE LESSONS

✓ Take out a sheet of paper and make a list of three to five habits you would like to develop or improve. How will your life be different once you adopt these productive habits?

✓ Next, write down the habits that are preventing you from achieving your goals. How are these habits holding you back?

✓ Identify at least three things you can do immediately to develop your new success habits. Enlisting the support of someone else to hold you accountable and reviewing your list daily are two ideas to get you started.

✓ Make it a regular practice to arrive early, use your million-dollar handshake, and write handwritten notes.

You can find more success habits at the *Life Lessons* blog:

www.lifelessonsthebook.com/blog

" THANKS FOR THE MEANING OF LIFE, BUT
I'LL STILL NEED MONEY. "

CHAPTER 7

ACHIEVE FINANCIAL INDEPENDENCE

I have been pondering what advice to give about money. What I keep coming up with is this: Do not act like typical Americans. Do not fail to save. Do not get yourself in debt up to your eyeballs. Work and take pride and honor from your work. Learn a useful skill that Americans really need, like law or plumbing or medicine or nursing. Do not expect your old Ma or Pa to always be there to take care of you. I absolutely guarantee that we will not be. Learn to be self-sufficient through your own contributions, as the saying goes. This advice has served me well. It was propounded to me by my late father, who often said, "Be prudent."

—BEN STEIN, AS QUOTED IN AN ARTICLE IN THE *NEW YORK TIMES*

TRINKETS AND TREASURES

When Dutch settlers came to the New World in 1626, they wanted to build a town on an island at the mouth of the Hudson River. Peter Minuit, a representative of the Dutch West India Company, negotiated a deal with Indians on the island to trade the land for some beads, cloth, and trinkets worth about 60 Dutch guilders, or approximately $24. The name of the island? Manhattan.

When you consider the worth of Manhattan's real estate today, it seems as if the Indians got the raw end of the deal. Before you jump to that conclusion, however, take a moment to consider the power of compound interest.

If they had taken their $24, invested it, and received 8% compounded interest, the Indians would have enough money today to buy all of Manhattan back. *And* they would have several hundred million dollars left!

No amount of money is too small to invest. What might seem like a nominal amount today can turn into a large amount of money over time, if you invest that money wisely.

THE PARABLE OF THE TALENTS

Again, it will be like a man going on a journey, who called his servants and entrusted his property to them. To one he gave five talents of money, to another two talents, and to another one talent, each according to his ability. Then he went on his journey. The man who had received the five talents went at once and put his money to work and gained five more. So also, the one with the two talents gained two more. But the man who had received the one talent went off, dug a hole in the ground and hid his master's money.

After a long time the master of those servants returned and settled accounts with them. The man who had received the five talents brought the other five. "Master," he said, "you entrusted me with five talents. See, I have gained five more."

His master replied, "Well done, good and faithful servant! You have been faithful with a few things; I will put you in charge of many things. Come and share your master's happiness!"

The man with the two talents also came. "Master," he said, "you entrusted me with two talents; see, I have gained two more."

His master replied, "Well done, good and faithful servant! You have been faithful with a few things; I will put you in charge of many things. Come and share your master's happiness!"

Then the man who had received the one talent came. "Master," he said, "I knew that you are a hard man, harvesting where you have not sown and gathering where you have not scattered seed. So I was afraid and went out and hid your talent in the ground. See, here is what belongs to you."

His master replied, "You wicked, lazy servant! So you knew that I harvest where I have not sown and gather where I have not scattered seed? Well then, you should have put my money on deposit with the bankers, so that when I returned I would have received it back with interest.

"Take the talent from him and give it to the one who has the ten talents. For everyone who has will be given more, and he will have an abundance. Whoever does not have, even what he has will be taken from him. And throw that worthless servant outside, into the darkness, where there will be weeping and gnashing of teeth."

—Matthew 25:14–30

The Frugal Millionaire

Laura Bickimer lived a simple life. Born and raised in Cleveland, Ohio, she taught math for 30 years before retiring in 1972. Bickimer never married, had no heirs, and lived in the same house where her parents had lived until moving into a nursing home in the final years of her life.

As a single woman, Bickimer was comfortable financially. She lived modestly, and once said she preferred to wash her clothes in an old-fashioned wringer, then hang them out to dry. Though frugal, even she was surprised when she discovered her net worth.

"My goodness," she said, "I'm a *millionaire!*"

The retired school teacher never earned more than $40,000 per year. But when she died in 2008, Bickimer left $2.1 million to her alma mater, Baldwin-Wallace College. As a teacher, and after her retirement, Bickimer's days were filled by learning and giving to others.

Explaining her strategy for daily living, Bickimer said, "I try each day to do some act of kindness or have some thoughtful communication that will bring happiness or perhaps enlightenment or solace to someone."

The Truth About Money

Growing up today is difficult when it comes to money. As a society, we are surrounded by grandiose promises about what our lives should look like. We are fascinated with the lives of the wealthy, which we hold up as models of success.

Television shows highlight celebrities and the ultra rich, and the inference is that we should all be living like that. During the 1980s and mid-90s, it was *Lifestyles of the Rich and Famous.* Host Robin Leach toured the playgrounds of the rich, featuring the extravagant lifestyles of wealthy entertainers, athletes, and business moguls. Leach concluded each episode with his signature phrase, "champagne wishes and caviar dreams."

Today, it's MTV's *Cribs,* which features tours of the houses and mansions of celebrities. The celebrities themselves get caught up in the hype, as several celebrities either have been accused or willingly used other people's homes and cars during the taping of the show, and claimed them as their own.

Stories abound of celebrities who at their peak earned more money than most people earn in a lifetime, and later found themselves in financial ruin. Four-time world heavyweight boxing champion Evander Holyfield and former *Tonight Show* sidekick Ed McMahon both lost their homes to foreclosure. Actor Nicolas Cage was hit with a multi-million-dollar tax lien from the Internal Revenue Service.

If celebrity status is not the ticket to long-term financial prosperity, neither is winning the lottery. Millions of people get sucked into the false hope that they will achieve financial independence by gambling, whether in casinos, at the racetrack, or by purchasing a lottery ticket at the local convenience store.

Even if you win big, your windfall provides no assurance of long-term financial success. Winners who don't know how to manage money before they win tend to enjoy a short windfall, followed by a downhill spiral that returns them to their prior financial condition, or worse.

One example of this is Andrew Jackson "Jack" Whittaker Jr. On Christmas Day, 2002, Whittaker stopped at a supermarket to purchase gas, a deli breakfast sandwich, and a Powerball ticket worth $315 million. The jackpot won by Whittaker was, at the time, the highest ever in the United States.

Over the next four years, Whittaker's life would completely unravel. He squandered his cash payment of $113.4 million, leaving a trail of destruction that included an arrest for drunk driving, unpaid casino debt in Las Vegas, and the death of his granddaughter by drug overdose.

We live in a time where there is more information than ever before about personal finance, and yet as a society we are missing these important lessons. No one would argue about the importance of education, and yet students aren't required to learn the basic life skill of money management. Because there is little or no formal training, kids learning about fiscal responsibility by observing families, companies, governments, and advertisers. The challenge is, those constituencies tend to model excessive spending, entitlement, and short-term gratification, without regard to the long-term consequences of that behavior.

When it comes to money, most people have it all wrong. Society, and the media, have painted a false picture of wealth—what it looks like, how it gets created, and where we fit in the picture. And we've swallowed that picture—hook, line, and sinker.

Guaranteed Financial Success

The good news is that financial success, and indeed financial *independence,* is available to everyone. You don't have to win the lottery, and you don't have to be a movie star. It doesn't matter if you are a teacher, a taxi driver, a waitress, or any other profession.

While conducting research for their book, *The Millionaire Next Door,* Thomas Stanley and William Danko discovered that, "It is seldom luck or inheritance or advanced degrees or even intelligence that enables people to amass fortunes. Wealth is more often the result of a lifestyle of hard work, perseverance, planning, and, most of all, self-discipline."

> *If you do rich people stuff, you get rich. If you do poor people stuff, you get poor. It's really that simple.*
>
> —Dave Ramsey

The people interviewed in Stanley and Danko's book were not entertainers and professional athletes. They were regular people, in regular careers. Their financial success was not determined by their career. It was determined by their *behavior* around money. Financial independence is not about *how much* money you make.

It's about *what you do with* the money you make, and how you live your life financially.

Achieving financial independence is not rocket science. It really boils down to just a few common sense strategies around money. It isn't always easy, because orienting your behavior to achieve financial independence requires "swimming against the tide" of societal norms. If you will do what most people are not *willing* to do, however, you will accomplish what most people are not *able* to do: You will achieve financial independence.

Live Within Your Means

This first strategy could also be entitled, "The only financial advice you'll ever need." In fact, I was tempted to write this chapter on money using only those four simple words. *Live within your means.* If this is the only thing you do, you will be far ahead of most people when it comes to money.

This is such a simple concept. Do not spend more

> *Spend less than you earn and do it for a long time, and you will be financially successful.*
>
> —Ron Blue

than you earn. And yet it's the biggest thing standing in the way of financial independence for most people in this country.

Too often people get caught up in a vicious cycle of going to work, earning money, buying stuff on credit, and then spending their paychecks to keep up with their burgeoning debt. Or, as their paychecks go up, so do their standards of living. They think, "I've worked hard, so I deserve to have more stuff or better stuff." And then they spend every penny they earn.

We live in a society that is heavily influenced by what everyone else is doing. For many, a great number of people's spending decisions are the result of their attempt to "keep up with the Joneses." In addition to the competitiveness with the people around them, television, magazines, catalogs, and other advertisements also influence their spending decisions. The irony is that many of the people around them—the Joneses of the world—are exposed to the same conditions. And most of the Joneses are living beyond their means, too.

Consider the following statistics:

- In a 2009 survey conducted by CareerBuilder.com, 61% of workers report they always or usually live paycheck to paycheck just to make ends meet. This means they are spending their entire paycheck (or more) each week, and are not saving any money. This is not strictly a function of income, either. Surprisingly, 30% of those who claimed to live paycheck to paycheck make more than $100,000 per year!

- About 40% of American families spend more than they earn, according to the Federal Reserve Board.

The gratification around overspending is short-lived, as the luster of the "shiny new toy" wears off very quickly. Like a drug addict who couldn't wait to get his next fix, the excitement of a new purchase fades over time. What doesn't go away, though, is the bill.

At best, you have the possessions you think you want, but you won't have any money in the bank. In the short run, no money in the bank means you'll be caught by surprise when emergencies arise. This could be as simple as needing a new set of tires, or having to pay an unexpected medical bill.

In the long run, it might prevent you from coming up with a down payment for a house, or sending your kids to college. You may not be able to retire when you want, or live comfortably during your retirement years.

Living above your means creates a tremendous amount of stress. Societal pressure to "keep up" is great, but it pales in comparison to the anxiety that results from buying stuff you can't afford. Instead of enjoying their toys, those who live beyond their means become slaves to their debt.

This financial stress pushes its way into other areas of life, such as health, work, and relationships. In fact, 57% of divorced couples in the U.S. cited financial problems as the primary reason for the demise of their marriage, according to a survey conducted by Citibank.

Cashing your check on Friday and having no money left at the end of the weekend is a formula for disaster, not a formula for long-term financial prosperity. Make the decision right now to live within your means.

This doesn't mean you can't ever treat yourself to a new toy, or splurge on something you've had your eye on for months. But you need to have the money to buy it. If you don't have the money, don't buy it. Period.

Avoid Debt

We are living during a time in human history where millions of Americans are suffocating in debt. Instead of living within their means, people are borrowing to finance their lifestyle. Once the cycle begins, it's very difficult to break. The only way to keep their consumptive lifestyle going is to borrow even more.

The most common form of debt is credit cards. They're easy to obtain, and the temptation to use them is very hard to resist. "Don't have the cash? Use plastic." This is the solution provided by credit card companies. And as a society, we're all too happy to comply.

According to *The Nilson Report*, 78% of households in the U.S. had one or more credit cards in 2009. Overall, consumers have an average of 5.4 cards. The latest figures from the Federal Reserve Board reveal that the average American household's credit card debt rose from $2,966 in 1990 to $9,840 in 2007. Credit card debt in the U.S. has reached a record high of nearly $1 trillion.

> *Borrowing money is like wetting your bed in the middle of the night. At first all you feel is warmth and release. But very, very quickly comes the awful, cold discomfort of reality.*
>
> —Elizabeth Gilbert

Americans, and consumers throughout the world, are financing their lifestyles with credit. This debt might take years to pay off, at a cost far in excess of the original purchase price.

Let's look at one example, using the Federal Reserve Board's statistics. If you paid the minimum (2%) payment on the average credit card debt in the U.S. ($9,840), at the average interest rate for a standard bank card (19% in March, 2007, according to cardtrack.com), it would take you 54 years to pay off your balance! During that time, you will have paid $34,590 in interest charges!

Debt is a trap—one that should be avoided at all costs. Nothing limits a person's ability to achieve financial independence more than having to make debt payments on a vacation taken two years ago, or clothes purchased last year that are now out of style, or shiny new toys that quickly depreciate in value.

In a survey of the Forbes 400 wealthiest people in the world, 75% said becoming and staying debt free was the most important key to building wealth. If you want to become better off financially—to achieve financial independence—you must stop buying things, especially the things you cannot purchase with cash. If you are in debt already, you must transition from a debt-dependent model to one based on savings and investment.

When I talk about the dangers of debt, I am speaking primarily about credit card and consumer debt. There are other kinds of debt—borrowing for education, obtaining a mortgage to buy a house, or investing in a business— that can be quite helpful, and allow us to do things that otherwise would not be possible.

Mortgages and other non-consumer debt don't get a "free pass," though. As this book is being written, we are in the midst of the biggest mortgage crisis in the history of the United States. The primary reason for this crisis is homeowners borrowing more than they could afford in order to purchase a home.

Additionally, many consumers are overextended with student loans. Kids today are leaving college with six-figure debt, especially if they go to law or medical school. How much you stand to earn in the future, and whether it will support the debt you incur, should always be carefully evaluated.

And business debt is not a panacea, either. With any debt, you must evaluate whether it makes economic sense to borrow the money, and you must always know how you're going to pay the money back.

In order to achieve financial independence, you must be free from the burden of debt. Here are a few practical strategies that will enable you to properly manage debt, rather than being controlled by the bondage of debt:

1. Stop borrowing money.

If you have no consumer debt, then resolve to stay debt-free. If you are burdened with debt currently, then stop the cycle right now. Make the decision to no longer use credit to finance your lifestyle.

2. Create a plan to eliminate your debt.

There are differences of opinion on how best to pay off credit cards and other consumer debt. Economically, you will get further ahead by paying off the highest interest debt first. Others recommend a strategy called the debt snowball method, where you pay off the accounts with the smaller balances first, and proceed to the larger ones later. What matters most is that you create a plan, and then follow that plan until you are debt-free.

3. When buying a house, get a 15-year mortgage instead of a 30-year mortgage.

By cutting the term of your mortgage loan in half, you will save tens of thousands of dollars in mortgage interest. While your payment will be higher, you will be far better off in the long run financially. If you currently have a 30-year mortgage, refinance to a 15-year mortgage as soon as possible.

4. Limit your mortgage payment to 25% of your gross income.

Don't ever take on mortgage debt with a payment that exceeds 25% of your gross income, regardless of what your mortgage broker says you can afford. Remember, mortgage lenders are in the business of selling loans. While they work within certain guidelines, lending more than borrowers could ultimately afford has wreaked financial havoc on thousands of people. Stay in control of your financial future by limiting the amount you borrow to what you can truly afford.

5. To get the best value for your money, avoid leasing cars, and instead buy a car that is between 24 and 30 months old.

When you drive a new car off the lot, it immediately depreciates 20% in value. It will depreciate another 8% the first year, and about 20% the second year. That's a total of almost 50% in the first two years. By purchasing a car that is 24 to 30 months old, you will maximize your purchasing power, and still be able to drive a reliable car with fairly low mileage. Buy a car you can afford, and pay cash if possible to avoid incurring debt.

Save Consistently

It doesn't matter how small the amount is. Sometimes, when you are just starting out, things are so tight it's hard to imagine saving any money whatsoever. But even if it's just $14 a week (the amount the average American spends weekly on coffee), get in the habit of saving consistently.

Saving consistently is essential to achieving financial independence. Creating a savings plan will allow you to save for short-term goals, such as a vacation, new furniture, or that home theater system you've always wanted.

In addition to saving for short-term goals, a portion of your savings should also be dedicated to long-term goals such as college, education, and retirement. It's important to set goals for each, and then create a plan to achieve your financial goals.

It's been said that there are about a half-dozen things that make all the difference in any area of our lives. Here are the six keys to saving consistently:

1. Start right away.

The best time to start saving for the future is when you're young. The second best time is *now*!

Why is it important to start saving right away? So you can tap into the power of "compound interest." Albert Einstein said this was mankind's greatest discovery, and called it "the eighth wonder of the world."

Compound interest is the amount of interest that is earned as additional interest is added to principal. As interest is added, the principal sum grows larger, resulting in even more interest.

Many people put off saving or investing until they "make more money," or "pay off their debt." But waiting can really hurt you. Consider the following example: Mark, who is 25 years old, begins saving $3,000 a year, but stops after only 10 years. Assuming an 8% return, his $30,000 investment will yield more than $472,000 by the time he reaches age 65.

Scott, on the other hand, doesn't start saving until age 35. He saves the same $3,000 per year, and continues investing for the next 30 years. Assuming the same rate of return, Scott will accumulate just $367,000. Even though Scott invested 20 years longer than Mark, he lost out on more than $100,000 because he waited to start saving.

2. Pay yourself first.

One of the biggest challenges for most people is, while they want to save money, they never seem to have anything left after paying all their bills. In order to build wealth, though, you must make the commitment to pay yourself first—*before* you pay any other bills. Decide on a certain amount, put that money into a savings or investment account, and then live on what's left over.

> *In the house of the wise are stores of choice food and oil, but a foolish man devours all he has.*
> —*Proverbs 21:20*

Not convinced you can do it? Sure you can! When people tell me they can't fit savings into their budget, I ask them what they would do if the federal government increased the tax rate, and more tax was withheld from their paycheck starting next week. "I'd be forced to pay it," they respond. Exactly.

3. Make saving automatic.

If you don't automate your savings and investing, you won't do it regularly. On the other hand, if you don't see it, you won't spend it. (Like our tax example in the previous section.)

If your company offers direct deposit, set this feature up immediately. Arrange to have a certain amount, such as $25 or $50 per week (or more if you can), taken out of your paycheck, and transferred into a savings account. If you are not able to take advantage of direct deposit at work, take a fixed amount or percentage out of each check, and put it into your savings account.

Saving is not just for adults, either. If you are a child, and you earn money babysitting, mowing the lawn, or doing odd jobs around the house or neighborhood, this is a great time to start your automatic savings plan. This applies to your allowance, too. Take a portion of all monies earned or received, and deposit it into a savings account.

Make it a goal to save at least 10% of your income for the rest of your life, starting today!

4. Build an emergency cash fund.

No matter how well prepared you are, unexpected financial needs will arise. The furnace goes out in the middle of January. Someone in your family gets sick, and the medical bills are not completely covered by your insurance company. You get laid off from your job.

If you haven't planned for the unexpected events, you are more likely to accumulate debt in order to meet your financial obligations. In the end, the cost of an unexpected home repair, for example, ends up significantly higher because of the interest paid over time on the debt.

With a little preparation, you can prevent these events from having a crippling, long-term effect on your finances. With a cushion, these unexpected financial needs will not turn into financial emergencies.

So how much money should you have in your emergency fund? Starting out, it can be as little as $100, especially if you are a student with few obligations. As a general rule of thumb, you should build up to three to six months of living expenses.

Keep your emergency cash fund in a separate savings account or high-yield money market fund. That way, it's not too easy to access, and you will earn interest on your money.

5. Contribute to a 401(k) or other retirement plan.

If you work for a company that offers a 401(k) retirement savings plan, arrange for a portion of your savings to go into that investment vehicle. Your 401(k) contributions are taken out before taxes, which provide additional, tax-deferred savings. And if your company offers a matching contribution, you receive "free" money that your employer contributes to your retirement savings.

For example, let's say your federal tax rate is 15%. If you contribute $10 to your 401(k), only $8.50 will be deducted from your check ($10.00 less the $1.50 tax savings). Assuming your company matches 50¢ per $1 contributed, your employer would contribute $5.00 on your behalf. The result: Your 401(k) contribution cost you $8.50, but a total of $15 was put into your account. That's what I call "return on investment"!

6. Increase your savings percentage over time.

Initially, your goal should be to save 10% of your gross income. If you're young and just starting out, then make this a "rule." If you're older, and not accustomed to saving, you may have to start smaller.

As your income increases, instead of increasing your lifestyle to meet your new income level, increase the amount you save and invest. Take half of your raise, and add that to savings or investments. You didn't have that money before, so you won't miss it. And if you are living within your means then you won't need it, either.

Follow that same strategy with any bonuses you might receive. Reward yourself with half of your bonus, and spend it on whatever you want. After all, you earned it, and you deserve it! But put the other half in your savings or investment account.

Give Generously

The topic of giving might seem out of place in a chapter about achieving financial independence. While topics like saving money and staying out of debt clearly contribute to financial freedom, giving money away seems to move us in the opposite direction, right?

> *God loves a cheerful giver.*
> —*2 Corinthians 9:7*

Sir John Templeton, the legendary mutual fund manager, provides great insight in this area. As one of the world's most successful investors, he was often asked the question, "What is the best investment?" His immediate response every time was "Tithing."

About the topic of giving, Templeton wrote:

"In all my fifty-two years before I retired as an investment counselor, we were helping people, literally hundreds of people, with their wealth. In all those years, there was only one investment which never proved faulty, and that was tithing—giving at least 10% of your income to churches and charities. In all my history, I have never seen a family who tithes for as long as ten years that didn't become both prosperous and happy. That is the best investment anyone can select."

Like other financial principles contained in this chapter, the concept of tithing finds it roots in the Bible. For Christians, tithing is a demonstration of faith. But even if you are not a Christ-follower, giving generously is an important part of achieving financial independence. In my opinion, if you don't understand and apply this concept, you will never have financial peace, which is the greatest gift that financial independence provides.

Give 10% of your income, starting today. The Bible indicates that this money goes to your local church. If you don't attend a specific church, then give this money to a non-profit organization you would like to help. There are people in need in your local community, and around the world. Find a cause you would like to support, and begin contributing to that organization.

If 10% is too much to start, then begin by giving *something*. Make a plan to increase the percentage over time, at least until you reach 10%. Remember Sir Templeton's words. While it might take a while to fully grasp the importance of giving generously, just know that every dollar you are contributing is helping someone else. Feel good about that, and trust that your generosity will not only impact others, but will change your life, too.

Create Multiple Streams of Income

In the workplace of the past, the bond between employers and employees was much stronger. There was tremendous loyalty on the part of both the employer and the employee. Employers provided a stable work environment, and employees worked their entire careers with the same company.

This may have been true in the 1950s, but the workplace has evolved since then. In an era where the only constant is change, there is less employment certainty than ever. According to *Business Week* magazine, the chances are one in three that you'll lose your job at least once during your working life. Studies show that the average working American will have three to five careers and between 10 to 12 jobs during his or her lifetime.

Self-employment is not a guaranteed ticket to long-term employment, either. According to the U.S. Small Business Administration, three out of every 10 new businesses survive only two years, and about half survive five years.

In spite of this uncertainty, most people are still relying on one source of income from their job or business. The problem with "placing all your eggs in one basket" is, if something happens to the basket, the result can be catastrophic.

Many of my friends in the automobile industry have learned this the hard way. They had created great lives for themselves, but their continued prosperity was dependent upon an ongoing need for automotive engineers. When the automotive industry was forced to make drastic cuts, these peoples' lives changed dramatically.

In order to achieve financial independence, you must create multiple sources of income. Additional sources of income provides:

- More money, which enables you to save and invest more.
- Diversification, in case one of your income streams is reduced or eliminated.
- Peace of mind, knowing that your financial condition does not depend on just one source.

Even with a full-time job, it's a good idea to have an extra source of income on the side. This could be rental real estate, a small business, or something as simple as selling things on eBay.

Always have a Plan B. In this case, additional sources of income would have reduced the impact of the global downsizing in the automotive industry.

Educate Yourself About Money

Unfortunately, most people don't usually learn about personal finance in school. While everyone is exposed to math, in many cases the math we learn ends up having little or no application in practical life.

For example, I took calculus in high school, as did many of my friends. Some of them truly needed this class, because it helped them prepare for the classes they took in college and, ultimately, their careers. But I never really "got" calculus. I was unable to grasp the concepts, and did poorly in the class.

> *You will either learn to manage money, or the lack of it will always manage you.*
>
> *—Dave Ramsey*

Once that year was over, I never had to solve another calculus equation in my life. Would the time I spent in calculus have been better spent learning something more practical? I often think so.

One of the best classes my children took in high school was business math. This class taught life skills that most people don't learn. Because they don't learn these skills, they have a difficult time navigating through their financial lives.

Our kids learned about the importance of a budget, and how to balance a checkbook. They learned about credit, as well as supply and demand. They learned how money works in the real world, and were introduced to practical skills they'll use the rest of their lives.

The more practical knowledge you accumulate, the better off you'll be financially. If your high school or college doesn't have a business math or personal finance class, you can easily educate yourself. Read books (see Suggested Reading at the back of this book), magazines (*Money, Kiplinger's, Personal Finance*), and newspapers (*Investor's Business Daily, Wall Street Journal*). Attend as many seminars and workshops as possible. Avail yourself of the many online resources, too.

> *An investment in knowledge always pays the best interest.*
>
> —Ben Franklin

It's also important to discuss finances with the people around you. Talk about money at the dinner table, with friends, and wherever else the topic comes up. Unfortunately, we live in a society that believes talking about money is "taboo." Don't buy into this perception. Instead, educate yourself—and help others, too—by talking about money with other people.

Regardless of your financial situation, you can always benefit from a financial education. If you're young, or not financially savvy, then this education is essential. Even if you're further along, though, you can always benefit from continuous learning in this area.

Wealth Is No Accident

As I said earlier in this chapter, achieving financial independence is not rocket science. If you will apply the principles in this chapter, you will achieve the peace of financial independence that eludes most people. Wealth is not an accident. Like success in other areas of life, it is the result of a few simple truths applied consistently over time.

> Earn all you can, save all you can, give all you can.
> —John Wesley

Make wise choices about how you will live your life financially. Create a plan, and follow that plan. If you stay the course, you will achieve peace, prosperity, and financial independence.

LIFE LESSONS

- ✓ Resolve today that you will live within your means and practice sound financial strategies, with the ultimate goal of achieving financial independence.

- ✓ Take out a piece of paper, and make a list of all your debt. If you don't have any, congratulations! Decide right now that you will never fall into the debt trap. If you have debt, make a plan for paying it off, so you can experience the freedom of being debt-free.

- ✓ Start saving money this week. Pay yourself first, and make savings an automatic part of your life. If you're already saving, I challenge you to increase your savings percentage.

- ✓ Make a list of financial goals that you would like to accomplish in the next 12 months, in 3 years, 5 years, and 10 years. Make a plan for achieving those goals, then do something every day, week, or month to move you toward your goals.

- ✓ Include giving in your financial goals. If you are not already contributing 10% of your income to your church, or to non-profit organizations, then make a list of what organizations you would like to support, and the steps you will take to accomplish that goal.

✓ Identify ways that you can earn additional income. Make a plan to diversify your income streams. Doing so will not only help you to save more and give more, but it will also provide diversification, in case one of your income streams is reduced or eliminated.

✓ Continue to educate yourself about money. There are many books that cover in greater detail the concepts found in this chapter. The more you educate yourself, the better off you will be financially.

Get more examples and tools to help you achieve financial independence at:

www.lifelessonsthebook.com

"Don't tell them we failed. Tell them we
decided to temporarily postpone our success."

CHAPTER 8

USE ADVERSITY TO PROPEL YOU FORWARD

"I have missed more than 9,000 shots in my career. I have lost more than 300 games. On 26 occasions I was trusted to take the game-winning shot, and I missed. I have failed over and over again in my life. And that is why I succeed."

—MICHAEL JORDAN, IN A COMMERCIAL FOR NIKE

THE ROAD TO SUCCESS IS PAVED BY FAILURE

Consider the track record of the person below:

    1831—Failed in business

    1832—Lost election in Legislature

    1833—Failed in business

    1836—Suffered a nervous breakdown

1838—Lost election for Speaker
1840—Lost election for Elector
1843—Lost election for Congress
1848—Lost election for Congress
1855—Lost election for Senate
1856—Lost election for Vice President
1858—Lost election for Senate

Our greatest glory is not in never falling, but in rising every time we fail.

—Confucius

Most ordinary people would not have persisted beyond the third or fourth failure. But the person who owns the track record above was no "ordinary" person. In 1860, after nearly three decades of "failure," Abraham Lincoln was elected as the 16th President of the United States.

PAINTING REJECTION

As an art dealer, he was a failure. During his lifetime, he was never recognized as a successful artist. His perseverance cost him a significant amount of money, physical strength, and perhaps even his sanity. Yet despite being knocked down again and again, Vincent Van Gogh never gave up his paint and brushes. He wrote to his brother, Theo:

"Although I find myself in financial difficulties, I nevertheless have the feeling that there is nothing more solid than a 'handicraft' in the literal sense of working with one's hands. If you became a painter, one of the things that would surprise you is that painting and everything connected with it is quite hard work in physical terms. Leaving aside the mental exertion, the hard thought, it demands considerable physical effort, and that day after day."

Van Gogh was subjected to rejection after rejection. Yet something in him refused to believe that he was a failure. He was an artist, and an artist painted. It was as simple as that. Van Gogh sold only one painting in his lifetime, "The Red Vineyard," which sold for a mere 400 francs just a few months before his death. Yet had he not persevered, the world would have missed the opportunity to enjoy such masterpieces as "Sunflowers" or "Starry Night," which today would demand more than $100 million.

OUTRUNNING DISABILITIES

Wilma Rudolph weighed just 4½ pounds when she was born. The 20th of 22 children, she spent most of her childhood in bed. Throughout her childhood, Wilma suffered from double pneumonia and scarlet fever. Then, when she was four years old, she contracted polio. She lost the use of her left leg, and doctors predicted she would never walk again.

Despite the doctors' prognosis, Wilma's mother, Blanche, was committed to doing whatever she could to help Wilma walk again. Once a week, Blanche would drive Wilma 90 miles roundtrip to a hospital for therapy. She massaged Wilma's leg every day, and even taught Wilma's brothers and sisters how to do it. Soon Wilma's crippled leg was being massaged four times per day.

Wilma wore a leg brace from the time she was five years old until she was nine. Then, one Sunday morning, she took it off, and walked down the aisle of her church.

> *The doctors told me I would never walk again, but my mother told me I would, so I believed my mother.*
>
> —*Wilma Rudolph*

"I spent most of my time trying to figure out how to get them off," she said. "But when you come from a large, wonderful family, there's always a way to achieve your goals."

By the time Wilma was 13, she played basketball and ran track at school. She was soon winning races, and was invited to a training camp at Tennessee State University. The track coach at Tennessee State, Ed Temple, became Wilma's most important professional influence.

In 1956, while still a sophomore in high school, Wilma Rudolph competed in the Olympic Games in Melbourne, Australia. At the age of 16, she was the youngest member of the U.S. team, and her sprint relay team won a bronze medal.

Wilma trained hard for the 1960 Olympics in Rome. Her hard work paid off, and she won the 100-meter, 200-meter, and 400-meter relay events. In doing so, she became the first American woman to win three gold medals in one Olympics.

Though she died in 1994 at the age of 54, Wilma Rudolph will always be remembered for her great determination. Her ability to overcome her physical disabilities is an amazing accomplishment, and a true inspiration.

Fear of Failure

Remember when you were a kid and you had no fear? Remember when, instead of having a million reasons why you *shouldn't* do something, you had a million reasons why you *should* do it? Remember when your relentless persistence caused you to do something over and over and over again, until you finally got it?

We all encounter adversity in life. We learn very quickly that things don't always go the way we want them to. We discover that, in spite of our best efforts, we sometimes fall short of our expectations. The label we often attach to this experience is "failure."

Failure can be a powerful and destructive force in our lives. Powerful in the sense that people often view failure as the final outcome. Destructive because the very fear of failure prevents so many people from accomplishing greatness in their lives.

How many times in your life have you not so much as attempted something, because of your fear of failing? Not even the failure itself, just the fear of it? That reaction is probably the natural human tendency. But it's also one of the main reasons people lose site of their goals and dreams. People dislike the taste of failure to such a degree that they would rather not try than fail.

> *A ship in the harbor is safe, but that is not what ships are built for.*
> —William Shedd

Don't be one of those people. If you are afraid to fail you won't try. And if you don't try, you won't know what you're capable of. By taking the safe path, you might not fail as often as those who try more things, but you are far less likely to achieve your full potential.

Instead of being afraid of failure, expect that it's part of the process. Accept that you will make mistakes along the way. And know in your heart that you will eventually succeed.

Learning From Adversity

Henry Ford once said, "Failure is the opportunity to begin again more intelligently." That's a wonderful approach to adversity—the idea that we can learn and grow even as we fall short of our desired outcome, and use those lessons as a way to improve in the future.

We certainly follow this prescription with children, don't we? During the potty training years, both infants and their parents experience the consequences of many "undesirable outcomes." Fortunately, this period does not continue indefinitely! Learning to ride a bike is another experience where children struggle at first, work through the frustration and the adversity, and eventually achieve their desired outcome.

Fall seven times. Stand up eight.
—Japanese proverb

When children take risks and fail, we show them that failure is not final, but rather provides an opportunity to regroup. We remain supportive, and encourage them to continue trying.

It's important that you do the same thing in your own life, too. It's inevitable that you will fall short of your expectations. Activities won't go as planned, you will take risks and fail, and you will become frustrated.

It's human nature at that point to want to give up. We all have the urge to throw in the towel after being faced with a certain amount of adversity and disappointment. When you are feeling the urge to give up—when you feel like you just don't have another try in you—remind yourself that quitters never win, and winners never quit. Use your adversity as an opportunity to learn and grow.

What can you do to learn from your failures? Every time you fall short, follow these five steps:

1. Don't exaggerate failures, or beat yourself up over them.

    Instead, accept them for what they are—a part of a process, a piece of the puzzle. Remember Napoleon Hill's belief that, "Every adversity, every failure, every heartache carries with it the seed of an equal or greater benefit." When you reframe failure in this way, it becomes possible not only to accept it, but to embrace it.

2. Don't blame others for your failures.

    It's human nature to blame anyone or anything other than yourself for your mistakes. But not taking responsibility for your mistakes robs you of the ability to learn from them. Be accountable for your failures and mistakes. Take ownership, so you can use your adversity as a stepping-stone.

3. Ask yourself what went wrong.

What caused the failure? What could you do to prevent the same outcome from occurring next time? Don't hesitate to ask others for their feedback and insight. Have you been turned down for a promotion time and time again? Ask your boss why.

> *Mistakes are the portals of discovery.*
> —*James Joyce*

Most people are willing to give constructive criticism when asked, but may be hesitant to give unsolicited advice.

4. Ask yourself what went right.

Spend as much time focusing on your strengths as you do on your weaknesses. Continue to do the things that are working.

5. Take action based on what you've learned.

Was your failure to get the promotion the result of lack of education? Then take the steps necessary to properly educate yourself. Was your failure to win the tennis tournament the result of a poor serve? Then work hard to improve your serve for next time. When you identify your reasons for failure, and then take appropriate action, you become better and your likelihood of success will increase.

One Step Closer to Success

Most people view failure as a final outcome. He fell short. She tried, but didn't succeed. He gave it his best shot, but didn't quite get it done. An author whose manuscript has been rejected might accept the publisher's decision as the fate for his book. He then shoves his manuscript in a drawer somewhere, never to be seen again.

Some people, however, view the event as simply a shortfall, evidence of the gap between the objective and the current reality. If you subscribe to this version, then you see failure as an opportunity for learning. You are able to evaluate what went wrong, as well as what didn't work as expected. You adjust your strategy, and then attempt it again.

> *Many of life's failures are people who did not realize how close they were to success when they gave up.*
> —*Thomas Edison*

The author whose manuscript has been rejected could say, "All successful authors are rejected at one time or another. This gives me an opportunity to evaluate what went wrong." Instead of letting the manuscript linger in a desk drawer, he makes changes, rethinks his strategy, and submits it again. A successful author goes through this process again and again—until his manuscript is ultimately accepted.

J.K. Rowling's *Harry Potter and the Sorcerer's Stone* was rejected by a dozen publishers, including many industry leaders, before a small London firm picked it up. Today, Rowling's seven-book series has sold more than 400 million copies, and has propelled Rowling to the status of one of the most successful women in the world.

There are many other authors who share Rowling's experience of being repeatedly rejected by publishers. Stephen King's *Carrie* was rejected dozens of times before finding a publisher, Margaret Mitchell's *Gone with the Wind* was rejected 38 times before acceptance, and renowned children's author Judy Blume endured two years of rejection notices before her first book was published. Think of what the world's readers would have missed out on had these authors not persevered!

This idea doesn't just apply to book publishing. It's not about the manuscript; it's about using adversity to propel you forward in *every* area of life. There are countless examples throughout history of people who have used "failure" to move one step closer to success:

- Babe Ruth is one of the greatest baseball players

> *I just keep goin' up there and keep swingin' at 'em. I know the old law of averages will hold good for me just the same as it does for everyone else.*
>
> —*Babe Ruth*

ever. He held the all-time home run record for years, before being passed by Hank Aaron. But what many don't know is that he also struck out more times than anyone in history—1,330 times!

- Thomas Edison had thousands of failures before he invented the light bulb. He firmly believed that each failed attempt led him closer to success.
- Dr. Seuss's first children's book, *And to Think I Saw It On Mulberry Street,* was rejected 27 times. The 28th publisher sold 6 million copies.
- Lucille Ball was kicked out of drama school for being too shy. She is now recognized as one of the most popular actresses of her era, and will long be remembered as "that crazy, loveable Lucy" from the hit television show, *I Love Lucy.*
- Henry Ford had several failed ventures before finally succeeding with Ford Motor Company. He went on to become one of the wealthiest and best-known industrialists in the world.
- Even after becoming completely deaf, Ludwig van Beethoven composed some of his most well-known and greatest works.

You can approach failure in two ways: you can either see your "strike outs" as the final outcome and label yourself a "failure," or you can view your "strike outs" as

> *Only those who dare to fail greatly can ever achieve greatly.*
>
> —*Robert F. Kennedy*

teachable moments—evidence that the law of averages will eventually tip in your favor. See failure for what it is—an outcome that builds character, and moves you one step closer to success.

LIFE LESSONS

- ✓ Think for a moment about your childhood. Which activities do you remember not being good at in the beginning, but later going on to master? What risks did you take, and what happened when you fell short of your expectations?

- ✓ Take out a piece of paper, and write down everything you learned from those childhood experiences.

- ✓ The next time you fall short, embrace it as part of the process. Remember that every outcome moves you one step closer to success.

- ✓ Now think about something you've wanted to do, but have been held back by fear of failure. What would you attempt to do if you knew you could not fail? Make a list of everything you need to do to accomplish that goal. Take one step immediately, and resolve to continue as long as it takes to succeed!

Don't Quit

When things go wrong as they sometimes will,
When the road you're trudging seems all uphill,
When the funds are low and the debts are high,
And you want to smile, but you have to sigh.
When care is pressing you down a bit,
Rest, if you must, but don't quit.

Life is queer with its twists and turns,
As everyone of us sometimes learns.
And many a failure turns about
When he might have won had he stuck it out.
Don't give up though the pace seems slow—
You may succeed with another blow.

Often the goal is nearer than
It seems to a faint and faltering man.
Often the struggler has given up,
When he might have captured the victor's cup.
And he learned too late when the night slipped down,
How close he was to the golden crown.

Success is failure turned inside out—
The silver tint of the clouds of doubt.
And you never can tell just how close you are;
It may be near when it seems so far.
So stick to the fight when you're hardest hit—
It's when things seem worst that you must not quit.

— Author unknown

"Nowadays, it's all about who you know, not what you know."

CHAPTER 9

SURROUND YOURSELF WITH SUCCESS

He who walks with the wise grows wise,
but a companion of fools suffers harm.

—PROVERBS 13:20

THE FARMER AND THE HORSE

A hardworking farmer needed another horse to help him plow his fields and pull his cart. So he called upon a local horse dealer.

"Please bring three horses to me," he said. "I'll evaluate them all, and will purchase the one I think is the hardest worker."

The next day the horse dealer brought three horses to the farmer. But instead of testing them at the plow or cart, the farmer merely opened the gate to his pasture, and allowed them to join his other horses. Two of the horses went to the right side of the field, where other horses were eating and sunning, while one horse went to the left side of the field, where the farmer's hardest-working mare was shielding a group of yearlings from the wind.

The farmer was immediately sure which horse he wanted. "I'll take that one," he said to the horse dealer, pointing to the horse who had joined the mare.

The horse dealer was astounded. The farmer had indeed picked the hardest working horse.

"How did you do that?" he asked. "You didn't even see the horses work."

"I don't need to," said the farmer. "I know that horse will be just like the one he chose as a friend."

HANGING OUT WITH BILLIONAIRES

Mark Victor Hansen, renowned co-author of *Chicken Soup for the Soul*, was lamenting to peak performance guru Anthony Robbins about his less than desirable level of success.

"I don't understand it," he said. "I just can't seem to get from where I am to where I want to be."

"Well, who are the people around you?" asked Robbins.

> *The next best thing to being wise is to live in a circle of those who are.*
>
> —C.S. Lewis

"That's the thing," Hansen replied. "I'm hanging out with millionaires."

"That's the problem," declared Robbins. "You need to start hanging out with *billionaires*."

Mark Victor Hansen took Tony Robbins' advice. The rest, as they say, is history.

CONVERSATIONS WITH TITANS

In 1908, an impoverished young journalist interviewed the wealthy industrialist, Andrew Carnegie. During the interview, Carnegie revealed that his formula of personal achievement was responsible not only for his great wealth, but for the wealth of all who learned this secret.

Carnegie was so impressed with the young journalist that he commissioned him to interview the successful men of the

> *If I have seen further it is by standing on the shoulders of giants.*
>
> —Isaac Newton

day, and then share their common denominators of success with the world. The journalist would receive no pay for his efforts, and Carnegie agreed only to provide letters of reference so the journalist could gain access to these well-known men.

For the next 20 years, the young journalist sat across from hundreds of well-known men—people like John D. Rockefeller, Thomas Edison, Alexander Graham Bell,

George Eastman, William Wrigley Jr., and Henry Ford—who had benefited financially and otherwise from the application of Mr. Carnegie's secret.

The journalist was Napoleon Hill, and the book documenting those interviews is *Think and Grow Rich*. Since it was published in 1937, millions of copies have been sold. The book remains one of the all-time bestsellers in its field.

Hill's book, one of the most influential books of all time in the area of success and personal achievement, was a direct result of the people he associated with. In fact, there's no way Hill would have learned the principles outlined in his book without surrounding himself with the wealthiest men of that era.

Be Careful Who You're Modeling

When I was growing up, I disagreed with my parents about a lot of things. Regardless of the outcome, one thing I never did was admit that they were right—about anything. While it's hard for me to acknowledge that in writing (I guess it's a "parent-child" thing), I realize now that they often *were* right. The story that follows illustrates one of those times.

Pete and I were close, starting in about seventh grade. We had many similar interests, not all of which were constructive. I remember our junior year in high school.

Pete and I had U.S. History together. Our teacher was Mr. Such, who I really liked. He had a handlebar mustache, and owned a cigar shop where he worked on the weekends and during the summer.

We always had homework in History, and Pete and I would sit in my basement bedroom working on it. Our homework often required lengthy essays. The thing was, Pete would sit there the whole time and do very little work. He waited patiently for me to finish, and then we would go out with our friends.

Looking back, I know it wasn't healthy for me to be friends with Pete. It's not that

> *Do not be misled: Bad company corrupts good character.*
>
> *—1 Corinthians 15:33*

he was a bad guy. It was more about how I was when I was with him. Let's just say I wasn't "achieving my full potential."

There were others, too. I don't mean to single out Pete. My parents seemed to know which friends were "good for me," and which ones weren't. Of course, I wasn't always receptive to their input. I felt, as teenagers often do, that I was better equipped to make that call than they were.

I was completely wrong about that. My parents were right. Fortunately, I learned that lesson. It was an important lesson to learn, because I believe it applies even more so in my life today. Why? Because the consequences of associating with the wrong people are greater today than they were when I was a kid.

> *If you lie down with dogs, you will get up with fleas.*
> —*English proverb*

When you surround yourself with great people, their habits, ideas, work ethic, and beliefs have a positive influence on you. To put it bluntly, if you associate with successful people, you'll become successful. If you associate with toxic, negative people, you are very likely to become toxic and negative yourself.

Evaluating Relationships

The great business philosopher, Jim Rohn, brilliantly articulates the importance of surrounding yourself with great people, and gives us sound advice on how to evaluate who we're around. Rohn provides three important questions that help us with this evaluation:

1. Who are you around?

Examine the people you spend the majority of your time with—your family, friends, acquaintances, and co-workers.

2. What are they doing to you?

What is the impact of your relationships with the people you're around? What activities are you engaged in when you're with them? What do you talk about? What do you think about? Are you growing as a person through your interaction with them?

3. Is that okay?

When looking at whether or not it's okay, here's the benchmark I use: Is this person supporting and expanding my ability to create the desired results in my life? Is he or she helping me to realize my full potential? For some people in our lives, the answer is clearly "yes." But if you're not sure, then it's time to take a closer look at these relationships.

The world is full of well-meaning people who, in spite of their desire to help, are not as supportive as you would like them to be. Sometimes, the people closest to you are the ones telling you all the reasons your idea won't work, or why your goals are unrealistic. The sooner you eliminate these toxic relationships, the better.

If it's not possible to completely remove yourself from certain relationships, at least minimize your time with those people. Rather than going out to lunch every day with your energy-draining, pessimistic colleague, restrict your contact to business matters only. If a good friend or a close relative is negatively impacting your life, then reduce your contact with them. Don't be mean, and don't reject them as people. Just move away from them, and do it quickly.

Finding Successful Role Models

Once you've adjusted your relationships with the people who are having a negative impact on your life, the next step is to expand the positive influences in your life. One way to accomplish this is by expanding your network. Just as Mark Victor Hansen and Napoleon Hill sought out successful people, you can do the same in order to learn from the success of others.

- **Join clubs and associations.** There's an organization for just about every profession and area of interest. Seek out the leaders in these organizations, those who are thriving in your field. Get to know them, and learn about their backgrounds. Ask them what advice they would give to someone looking to emulate their success. Watch what they do, and how they do it. Then, try to incorporate their success habits into your own life.

- **Take classes and seminars.** When you take classes and seminars, you are usually surrounding yourself with people who want to be the best at what they do. Otherwise, they would not be investing their time and money to improve themselves. Classes and seminars provide an opportunity not only to learn, but also to develop relationships with like-minded people.

- **Find a mentor.** In his book *Outliers: The Story of Success,* Malcolm Gladwell concludes that it takes about 10,000 hours to become an expert at something. If you are fortunate enough to find a mentor, you can shorten your learning curve dramatically.

  The support of an experienced person in your field is like having a key that unlocks the secrets to success. A mentor will not only show you the critical success factors in your field, but will also reveal the pitfalls to avoid. As a

  > *As iron sharpens iron, so one man sharpens another.*
  > —*Proverbs 27:17*

  trusted confidante and advisor, a mentor can provide valuable feedback and guidance. The support of a mentor can have a profound impact on your career, and on your life.

  As you interact with successful role models, think about the people you are asking for advice. Get to know them, and explore the possibility of working together in a more formal, mentorship structure. Once you hit it off with someone, this type of relationship will often evolve naturally.

- **Hire a coach.** If you aspire to become a professional tennis player, then you'll definitely want to join the USTA, read books and articles about tennis, and attend tennis classes or seminars. But to have any chance of rising to the top, you would need to do one more thing—hire a personal coach. While you could improve on your own by practicing, watching the top players, and modeling their strokes and strategies, a coach would help you in ways that you could simply not learn on your own.

If you're serious about working out, then hire a personal trainer. If you want to learn to play the piano, then hire a piano teacher. If you're looking to improve the bottom line in your business, then hire a business coach. And if you want to achieve greater success in your life, then hire a success coach!

A coach or other professional can help you take your "game" to the next level. Just ask tennis player Roger Federer, or golfer Phil Mickelson. For any area of life you might want to improve, there are people who can help you do it faster, easier, and with greater predictability than you could on your own.

> *The quality and quantity of your contacts and your relationships will have more to do with your success than perhaps any other factor. Knowing the right people and being known by them can open doors for you that can save you years of hard work.*
>
> —*Brian Tracy*

If you're truly serious about achieving excellence in your life, then make this important investment in yourself. You will be amazed by the difference it will make in your life!

Your Environment Counts

When you think about the idea of "surrounding yourself with success," another important area to focus on is your environment. The music you listen to, the books you read, the television shows you watch, and the media you are immersed in all have a huge impact on your success.

Just as you are committed to surrounding yourself with people who have a positive impact on you, make sure you also choose an environment that helps you to be your best. Look at your life in terms of your environment. Are the things around you positively impacting your life, or are they negatively impacting you? Eliminate everything that's holding you back, and surround yourself with an environment that helps you to be your best.

The people you are around, and the environment in which you live, have a tremendous impact on your long-term success in life. The old adage, "If you want to be successful, study everything that successful people do, and do the same thing," is oversimplified, but true. Choose wisely, and surround yourself with success. Doing so will rapidly accelerate the pace at which you achieve your goals.

Be Someone Others Want to Be Around

We've spent a lot of time in this chapter talking about the importance of spending time with the right people. It's equally as important to be the type of person that others want to be around.

Why? Just as you are seeking positive and successful influences, so are others. If you aren't the type of person that others admire, it will be very difficult to attract the kind of successful people you're seeking. So take a look at your behavior and actions, and ask yourself a simple question: "Am I the type of person that others want to be around?"

> *We could all use a little coaching. When you're playing the game, it's hard to think of everything.*
> —*Jim Rohn*

Author Rusty Berkus said, "There comes that mysterious meeting in life when someone acknowledges who we are and what we can be, igniting in us the circuits of our highest potential." Be the best person that you can be, and you'll attract those who will help you reach your highest potential.

LIFE LESSONS

✓ Take out a sheet of paper and make a list of the ten people you are around the most. What impact are they having on your life? What will you do as a result of your answer?

✓ Identify at least three ways you can surround yourself with successful people. Take one action immediately to seek out positive influences in your life.

✓ Think about the effect your environment is having on your life. Discipline yourself to do everything you can to create a positive environment around you.

For more ways to surround yourself with success, go to:

www.lifelessonsthebook.com/blog

"At Survival Camp, I learned how to
make an iPod from mud and twigs!"

CHAPTER 10

NEVER STOP LEARNING

In a time of drastic change it is the learners who inherit the future. The learned usually find themselves equipped to live in a world that no longer exists.

—ERIC HOFFER

NEVER TOO OLD

In April of 1930, nineteen-year-old Nola Ochs took her first college course at Ft. Hays State University in Hays, Kansas. It was a correspondence course called *Directed Study*.

But Nola's college career was short-lived. As was the case for so many women during that period in history, life intervened and college was pushed to the back burner. Nola got married and had children. As a wife and mother, she guided her family through the dustbowl and difficult financial times. She became a grandmother, and then a great-grandmother.

Nola had plenty to do to keep the family farm running smoothly, but her yearning to learn never left her. So when her husband died in 1972, Nola, then 61 years old, decided to head back to school and began, once again, taking correspondence courses. Her goal? To earn her bachelor's degree.

After taking a class here and there through the years, Nola found herself close to having an undergraduate degree. During her last year of college, her "senior" year, she moved into a dorm for non-traditional students at Ft. Hays State and took classes on campus.

> *I don't dwell on my age. It might limit what I can do. As long as I have my mind and health, it's just a number.*
>
> —Nola Ochs

In 2007, at the age of 95, Nola Ochs walked up onto the stage at Ft. Hays' graduation to receive her diploma. In addition to earning her degree, Nola also earned a spot in the *Guinness Book of World Records* as the oldest person to ever finish college.

Although her world record was short-lived—a 96-year-old man in Taiwan broke the record in 2009—Nola went on to receive her master's degree in 2010. After a college career that spanned 80 years, Ochs intends to apply for a graduate teaching position in Ft. Hays State's history department.

A One Woman-Show

She is a comedienne, best-selling author, Tony-nominated actress, and playwright. She has written screenplays, authored columns and given lectures, and has been a syndicated radio host. You've seen her interviewing other celebrities on the red carpet, as well as selling her jewelry and skin care lines on television. No doubt, Joan Rivers is one of the most successful women in show business.

> *What's my advice for kids today? Work like a dog, and education, education, education. . . . If you want it enough, you make it happen.*
>
> —*Joan Rivers*

But it hasn't been easy. The daughter of Russian immigrants, Rivers worked very hard to become a successful comedienne. And she has evolved from there, over a career that spans decades. Knowing that other comediennes tend to fade out after reaching a certain age, Rivers is not willing to suffer the same fate. So she continues to adapt and reinvent herself to survive in the ever-changing world of celebrity.

Rivers has morphed from comedienne to red carpet mainstay to fashion authority. How has she done this? By continually learning, evolving, and changing. Rivers has kept her finger on the pulse of the latest trends in art, jewelry, and fashion, and positioned herself as an authority in these areas. She leveraged this expertise by developing her own jewelry line. When Rivers realized that others looked up to her as someone who was aging gracefully, she did the research to develop her own skincare line, which was sold on QVC.

Joan calls herself "one of the hardest working women in the world," and who knows where we will see her next!

ANCORA IMPARO

The elderly man sat quietly, reflecting on his long life. After pondering all he had accomplished during his 87 years, he pulled out his sketchbooks. Page by page, he reviewed the archives of his life. After contemplating his work for some time, he wrote the words "Ancora Imparo" in one of the books. The phrase, translated from Italian, means "I am still learning."

> *My greatest wisdom is the knowledge that I do not know.*
>
> —*John Steinbeck*

Years later, when the sketchbook and its scrawling were discovered, the words "Ancora Imparo" became a motto for those dedicated to lifelong learning. Why? Because the words were written by Michaelangelo. Despite all he had accomplished, including such remarkable masterpieces as the Sistine Chapel and David, Michelangelo still found delight in the opportunity to learn.

Unprecedented Change

The world is constantly changing and evolving. And it's been this way since the beginning of time. Heraclitus, the Greek philosopher, said, "There is nothing permanent except change." To achieve success in a constantly changing world, you have to adapt to change with it. And in order to do that, you must be willing to continually learn.

This is true not only for individuals, but also for businesses. For example, the advent of the Internet has completely changed the

> *The only skill that will be valuable in the 21st century is the ability to learn new skills.*
>
> —*Peter Drucker*

way businesses reach their customers. It used to be that a company told a potential customer about its product or service through a print, radio, or television ad. But today, customers search for information using their computers. They can find a wide range of opinions on a product or service through blogs, chat rooms, and social media sites. Companies that wish to remain successful must change the way they do business. And in order to do that, they must continue to learn.

Commit to Lifelong Learning

When it comes to change, there are essentially three kinds of people: those who make things happen, those who watch things happen, and those who look around and say, "What happened?" If you want to be part of the first group—those who make things happen—you'll need to commit to lifelong learning.

When I say "learning," I'm not talking about academic learning. While academic learning certainly has its place, what I'm referring to is ongoing self-improvement. Our world is changing faster than ever before. If you're not constantly learning to keep up with it, you'll be left in the dust.

> *It's what you learn after you know it all that counts.*
>
> —*John Wooden*

Change creates opportunity, and those who are willing and able to learn new skills will be well positioned to benefit from change. By improving your skills, you set yourself up to take advantage of any opportunities that arise. History is full of successful people who were committed to lifelong learning:

- Grandma Moses did not begin painting until she was 70 years old, and received no formal training. As a self-taught painter, she became one of the world's most famous folk artists.
- David Bowie had only a few singing and saxophone lessons in the 1960s. He would later teach himself to play the piano, guitar, harmonica, and drums.

- Albert Einstein's ideas, published in 1905, lacked a bibliography, because they were generated by himself, based on what he had learned.
- Jose Saramango, winner of the Nobel Prize for Literature, was an unschooled locksmith who taught himself how to write.
- Because of his behavioral problems, famous poet and artist William Blake never received formal schooling. Instead, he took learning into his own hands, and devoured books on a variety of subjects.

Invest in Yourself

The best investment you can make is an investment in yourself. Investing in yourself means doing what it takes to ensure you have the skills, knowledge, and tools for optimal success. This used to be optional, especially a couple of decades ago when the trend was to start at one organization, work your way up the ladder, and retire with a nice gold watch. In today's fast-paced society, however, this is no longer the case. You are either moving forward or backward—there is no status quo.

You will talk to people who don't believe they can afford it. This couldn't be further from the truth. The fact is, they can't afford *not* to invest in themselves.

You will also run into people who believe continuous learning makes sense for others, but not for them. They think they already know everything they need to know. Don't be fooled by their false logic. No matter how long you've been in business, investing in your own personal and professional development will help you stay at the top of your field.

The bottom line is this: If you are not constantly learning and growing, then you have only yourself to blame when you get left behind. Make the decision now to invest in your own personal development.

1. Read one hour per day.

Read something every day in your chosen field, or in some area of personal development, or both. If you will do this for one hour per day, you will become an expert in your field in just three years.

I am a voracious reader, and I recommend that you do the same. In addition to periodicals and books related to your career, read outside your area of interest, too.

> *You will be the same person in five years as you are today except for the people you meet and the books you read.*
>
> —*Charlie "Tremendous" Jones*

I had an experience a while back that showed me just how valuable it could be to read outside your normal area(s) of interest. I was perusing the magazine section of our local library one Sunday afternoon. Instead of heading toward my usual fare—business, investing, personal development—I picked up *ARTNews*. The cover story, titled "ARTNews 100," covered the 100 largest private art collectors in the country.

I was captivated by the story of Donald Hess, a Swiss multimillionaire with two passions—wine and contemporary art. Hess has an amazing art collection, and he chose to house it in a winery built in 1903. Because he believes it is the responsibility of the collector to ensure that art is seen by the greatest number of people possible, he opened the Hess Collection Winery in 1989.

Most homes valued at over $250,000 have a library. That should tell us something.

—Jim Rohn

The timing was uncanny as my wife, Heidi, and I were leaving for Napa in two weeks. We visited the Hess Collection at a winery that today remains one of my favorites, because of the amazing art collection that is housed there. Had I not picked up a magazine outside my area of interest, we would have never discovered this gem.

I don't want to leave the subject of reading without talking about the greatest book of all time, the Bible. For Christians, the Bible is the how-to manual on living your life the way God intended. If you are a Christ-follower—and even if you're not—consider including the Bible in your daily reading time.

2. Listen to audio programs.

Even if your commute to work is just 15 minutes one way, you will be in your car for 125 hours per year. This is the equivalent of three 40-hour workweeks. And most people have even longer commutes.

Imagine what would happen if you turned your car into a "university on wheels," and invested that time in your personal growth. Rather than listening to talk radio or music, you can continue to develop your expertise in your chosen career, or in another area of interest.

> *Stockbroker presents an opportunity. When you say "no," you're really saying, "I don't think it's a good investment." When you refuse to read books, listen to audio programs, and attend seminars, you're really saying, "I don't think I'm a good investment."*
>
> —*Brian Tracy*

3. Attend seminars, workshops, and classes.

It takes hundreds, and sometimes thousands, of hours to create a seminar, workshop, or class. When you attend one, you are able to benefit from someone else's efforts to distill the most important information on that topic. Events are offered for every subject imaginable, and the information learned can have a tremendous impact on your life.

4. Utilize online technology to learn at home.

Thanks to technology, you can now earn degrees and certifications online, or simply take a class in a subject area that interests you. The access to formal online education is virtually unlimited. This is a great solution for those who need a bit more flexibility—such as the full-time working professional or the stay-at-home mom—and for anyone who prefers to learn in the comfort of their own home.

Finally, remember to learn from life, too. It's not all about what you learn from books and seminars. Some of the greatest lessons you'll learn will come from your own life experiences. Take note of your failures. Take note of your successes. And apply what you learn as you go through life.

Work on Your Skills Every Day

What do you think will happen to the marathon runner who suddenly stops training? Chances are, he won't be able to finish the marathon. Well, learning is a lot like running marathons. If you don't keep training, you'll lose the benefits you worked so hard to gain.

> *Formal education will make you a living; self-education will make you a fortune.*
> —*Jim Rohn*

Make a commitment to learn for one hour every day, seven days per week. By the end of the year, you will have accrued 365 hours of "classroom" time. Because so few people make a commitment to lifelong learning, you'll be way ahead of your competitors—and well on your way to realizing your dreams and goals.

LIFE LESSONS

✓ Make a list of everything you can do to become an expert in your field in the next three years. What books can you read? What audio programs are available? What seminars, workshops, or courses can you attend?

✓ Review your list, and create an action plan for continuous learning. Set deadlines, then do something every day that will move you toward your goal. Whenever you see something that will help you, add it to your list.

The *Life Lessons* website is a great support structure for continuous learning. Get more examples and tools today at:

www.lifelessonsthebook.com.

"You're spending the best years of your life doing a job
that you hate so you can buy stuff you don't need to
support a lifestyle you don't enjoy. Sounds crazy to me!"

CHAPTER 11

REALIZE THAT THE BEST THINGS IN LIFE AREN'T THINGS

To laugh often and much, to win the respect of intelligent people and the affection of children, to earn the appreciation of honest critics and endure the betrayal of false friends, to appreciate beauty, to find the best in others, to leave the world a bit better, whether by a healthy child, a garden patch, or a redeemed social condition . . . to know even one life has breathed easier because you have lived. This is to have succeeded.

—RALPH WALDO EMERSON

BIG ROCKS

I was on vacation with my wife and children in Florida, and as I sat at the edge of the pool watching my children swim, I thought about what a blessing it was to be enjoying our wonderful time together. As I reflected on the importance of "family time," I was reminded of Dr. Stephen Covey's story about "big rocks." Here's the story, which Covey tells in his book, *First Things First:*

In the middle of a seminar on time management, a lecturer decided to quiz the audience. Reaching under the table, he pulled out a wide-mouthed gallon jar and sat it on the table next to a platter covered with fist-sized rocks. "How many of these rocks do you think we can get in this jar?" he asked.

After the students made their guesses, the seminar leader said, "Okay, let's find out." He put one rock in the jar, then another, then another—until no more rocks would fit. Then he asked, "Is the jar full?"

Everyone could see that not one more of the rocks would fit, so they said, "Yes."

"Not so fast," the teacher cautioned. From under the table he lifted out a bucket of gravel, dumped it into the jar, and shook it. The gravel slid into all the little spaces left by the big rocks. Grinning, he asked once more, "Is the jar full?"

A little wiser by now, the students responded, "Probably not."

"Good," the teacher said. Then he reached under the table to bring up a bucket of sand. He started dumping sand in the jar. While the students watched, the sand filled the little spaces left by the rocks and gravel. Once more he looked at the class and asked, "Now is the jar full?"

"No!" everyone shouted back.

"Good!" said the seminar leader, who then grabbed a pitcher of water and began to pour it in the jar. He got something like a quart of water into that jar before he said, "Ladies and gentlemen, the jar is now full. Can anybody tell me the lesson you can learn from this?"

An eager participant spoke up: "Well there are gaps in your schedule. And if you really work at it, you can always fit more into your life."

"No," the leader said. "That's not the point. The point is this: if I hadn't put those big rocks in first, I would have never gotten them in."

A DYNAMITE LEGACY

In 1888, a man opened the newspaper to the obituary section to read about his beloved brother, who had just passed away. But one headline immediately caught his eye. It read: "The Merchant of Death is Dead."

It was the obituary of Alfred Nobel, an armaments manufacturer and the inventor of dynamite. The article continued, "He became rich by finding ways to kill more people faster than ever before. And yesterday, he died."

While many readers were shocked by the caustic words in that obituary, the man having breakfast in Cannes, France, was probably the most shocked of all. Because "the man" was Alfred Nobel, and he was very much alive.

The writer had confused Alfred with his younger brother, Emil. Alfred had been developing nitroglycerine as an explosive, and his experiments caused an explosion that killed five people, including his own brother.

Even more distressing to Alfred was how he was portrayed in the article. Is this how people saw him? Alfred invented dynamite for the building and mining industries, as a means of reducing the cost of drilling tunnels, blasting rocks, and building bridges. As an inherently peaceful man, he was saddened that it had later found another use in wars.

As Alfred mourned the death of his younger brother, he reflected on his own legacy—how he would be remembered after he died—and the impact his invention of dynamite would have on the world.

When Alfred died eight years later, his will provided for the establishment of the Nobel Prizes. His fortune funded five "prizes" to be awarded annually. They recognized achievements in physics, chemistry, physiology or medicine, literature, and peace. Each prize included a cash award that today exceeds one million dollars.

Alfred Nobel's erroneous obituary provided a second chance—the opportunity to create a legacy that would make a positive impact in the world. Instead of buying "things" with his fortune, Nobel invested in people. That investment has made the world a significantly better place.

An Hour of Your Time

A father came home from work late. He was tired, and irritated to find his seven-year-old daughter waiting for him at the door.

"Daddy, may I ask you a question?" asked the girl.

"Sure," said the father.

"How much do you make per hour?" his daughter asked.

Treat the people in your life as though they were the most important people in the world, because they are.

—Brian Tracy

The father thought the answer was none of her business, but he answered the question anyway. "If you must know, I make $50 per hour," he said.

"Okay," said his daughter. "Can I borrow $25?"

That made the father furious. "If you want to borrow money for some silly toy or other nonsense, then you march yourself straight to your room and think about why you are being so selfish. I don't work hard every day so you can clutter your room with more stuff!" The little girl went quietly to her room and closed the door.

After about an hour, the man started to calm down. After all, his daughter never asked for money. Perhaps he had overacted. The man went to his daughter's room, and opened the door.

"I've been thinking that maybe I was too hard on your earlier," the father said to the girl, reaching for his wallet. "Here's that $25 you asked for."

"Thank you Daddy!" the little girl exclaimed. Then, reaching under her pillow, she pulled out some crumpled bills. The girl began to count out her money.

But the father was starting to get angry again. "Why did you ask me for money if you already had some?" he asked.

"Because I didn't have quite enough," the girl said. "I have $50 now. Can I buy an hour of your time? Please come home early tomorrow. I would love to have dinner with you."

The father was crushed. With tears rolling down his cheeks, he wrapped his arms around his beautiful daughter and told her how sorry he was. In that moment, the girl's father realized the company he worked so hard for could replace him in a matter of minutes . . . but he could never be replaced as a father.

The Lines Have Blurred

Continuing with Dr. Covey's metaphor, we all have big rocks, gravel, sand, and water in our lives. The natural tendency seems to favor the gravel, sand, and water, leaving little space for the big rocks. In an effort to respond to the "urgent," the "important" is often set aside.

To be sure, creating a balanced life is more challenging than ever before in human history. There are more demands than ever on our time, and the line between work and personal life has faded.

Part of the difficulty can be attributed to the way we use technology. Devices such as cell phones and laptops definitely give us more flexibility. You are now able to leave the office a little earlier to attend your child's sporting event, because you can chat with a client on your cell phone en route to the game.

> *Think of life as a game in which we juggle five balls labeled Work, Family, Health, Friends, and Integrity. One day, you understand Work is a rubber ball. You drop it and it bounces back. The other four balls are made of glass. Drop one of those, and it will be irrevocably marked, scuffed, nicked, and maybe even shattered.*
>
> *—James Patterson*

But technology has also tethered us to our work. How many times have you seen a mother working on her laptop

> *"Life moves pretty fast.
> If you don't stop and look
> around once in a while,
> you could miss it."*
>
> —*Ferris Bueller, in the
> movie* Ferris Bueller's
> Day Off

at your son's basketball game, or a dad talking on his cell phone while dining with his family at a local restaurant? How many times have *you* done something like this?

Technology is not the only culprit, however. For many people, work has become a "big rock," leaving little room for other areas of their lives—their families, friends, health, and happiness. This is occurring for a couple of reasons:

- With smaller staffs expected to do the same amount of work, people find themselves working crazy hours simply to keep their heads above water and keep their jobs. Because the traditional 9 to 5 day is a thing of the past, people are having a harder time putting limits on how much they work.
- Work provides the satisfaction of meeting challenges and goals. The structure of work, its clear feedback system, and the ability to "accomplish" often seems lacking at home. For example, if you close a big sale at work, chances are you'll be lauded, will earn additional money, and may even receive a promotion. Spending an afternoon at the beach with your family, by comparison,

might not bring the same recognition. The "accomplishment" is not so obvious, and the rewards are not as evident and concrete.

- The lines have blurred, and it's now easier than ever to work at home, and play at work. The problem is, this lack of separation, or "balance," deteriorates the quality of life in both areas. The unfortunate result is that the issues at home are more difficult to resolve, and you potentially trade work success for quality of life with the most important people in your life.

Someone once observed, "No one on their death bed wishes they had more time in the office." Unfortunately, it often takes a deathbed (or similar) experience for this realization to set in.

Achieving Balance

Achieving balance requires true effort and commitment. At first you'll have to consciously schedule time for yourself, your family, and friends. You may have to fight the urge to do something "more important." For some, "personal time" can seem frivolous. But in reality, spending time with the people you love is the best way to leave your imprint on them—and on the world.

There's no better way to leave the world a better place than to transfer your values and integrity to your children, friends, co-workers, and other people who are important to you. In the grand scheme of things, this is infinitely more important than anything you could possibly do at work. And while you may not receive immediate accolades, when all is said and done your life will be much more satisfying if you cultivate meaningful relationships with those around you.

The following steps can help you effectively manage your life, and achieve a more fulfilling balance between work and your personal life:

1. Make time for others.

Structure your schedule so you have time for the most important people in your life. Unless you are intentional about time with your spouse, children, friends, and others, you will look back on your life and realize that much of your time was expended in less important areas.

> *Remember, you can earn more money, but when time is spent it is gone forever.*
>
> *—Zig Ziglar*

Commit to being involved in your children's activities. Remember, kids spell love T-I-M-E. If you can't be a coach or a group leader, at least take time to attend games or other important events. You will soon forget whatever you sacrificed to get to the game, but your children will always remember that you were there.

Make time for your spouse, too. If you're like me, your spouse seems to get whatever is left over at the end of the day—and sometimes there's nothing left! My relationship with Heidi has been best when we've been intentional about scheduling time alone with each other. Date nights are one way to make sure you're investing quality time with your spouse.

How about just sitting down at the dinner table together as many nights as possible? Sharing a meal together is a great way to connect and keep in touch with what's going on in each other's lives.

Commit to being involved in the lives of the people you love. It's one of the best investments you'll ever make!

2. Make time for yourself.

While it's important to invest in others, it's just as important to invest in yourself. Exercising, learning about something you are interested in, working on a hobby, or enjoying a great book in your favorite reading chair are all ways that you can invest in yourself. Doing so will renew your mind and body, and provide more energy for the other demands in your life.

When I travel on a plane, the flight attendant always describes the emergency procedures. He or she instructs the passengers to put on their own oxygen mask before helping others. This is important not only when the cabin pressure is lost on a plane, but also in life. Make sure that "self-care"—taking care of yourself—is one of your "big rocks."

3. Take time to "get away from it all."

Vacations are a great way to re-energize, and they serve as a reminder that there's more to life than just work. Vacations can take many forms: An overnight stay with your spouse at a hotel in the area, a weekend away with your family, or a dream vacation that you and your family have been planning for months. Occasionally, I'll even travel with just one of my children, for a special "daddy-daughter" or "daddy-son" trip.

For great ideas on places to go and things to do, read books like *1,000 Places to See Before You Die* or *100 Best Vacations to Enrich Your Life*. Not only will you get specific ideas for wonderful trips, but these books will also cause you to think of other exciting possibilities for you and your family.

Vacations don't have to be expensive, either. Camping is a great way to get away, and is relatively inexpensive. It's also fun, and much easier, to plan activities in your community, or even at home. You can have just as much fun playing cards or a board game at home, or visiting local attractions in the area.

4. Finally, treat each day as a gift from God.

Ask yourself how, when you look back on your life, this day will matter. Remember that the best things in life aren't things, and make a conscious effort to live your life in a way that meaningfully impacts the most important people in your life.

In the jar that is *your* life, be sure to put the "big rocks" in first. When you do that, there will be plenty of room for the gravel, the sand, and the water.

LIFE LESSONS

✓ Make a list of the most important people in your life. If you only had one month to live, who are the people you would want to spend time with?

✓ Resolve today that you are going to spend more time with the people you love.

✓ Schedule "appointments" with your children, spouse, and friends. Plan a "Family Night," make reservations for dinner, or book a vacation.

✓ Make a habit of doing this regularly for the rest of your life. Put the "big rocks" in first, and demonstrate your commitment to the most important people in your life.

"There's war, disease, poverty, and violent crime all over the world...and your greatest concern is me not eating peas!"

CHAPTER 12

MAKE A DIFFERENCE

*You are not here to merely make a living. You are
here in order to enable the world to live more amply,
with greater vision, with a finer spirit of hope and
achievement. You are here to enrich the world, and
you impoverish yourself if you forget the errand.*

—WOODROW WILSON

A CELEBRITY GIVES BACK

He acted in more than 65 movies, during a career that
spanned five decades. He was nominated 10 times for an
Academy Award, and then won the award for best actor
after his performance in 1986 film, *The Color of Money.* He
won three Golden Globe Awards, a Cannes Film Festival
Award, an Emmy award, and numerous other awards.

He was also an auto-racing enthusiast. After playing
a race car driver in the movie *Winning,* he took up racing

for real. He won several national championships in road racing, and his teams won several championships in open wheel IndyCar racing. At the age of 70, he became the oldest driver to be part of the winning team in a sanctioned race, the Rolex 24 Hours of Daytona.

His acting career and his success as a racecar driver were impressive, to be sure. But the biggest impact Paul Newman made, and what he will likely be remembered for most, was in his philanthropic efforts.

Newman founded Newman's Own, a line of food products, in 1982. Starting with a salad dressing given to friends and family during the holidays, the brand has expanded to include pasta sauce, lemonade, popcorn, salsa, and wine. Newman established a policy that all proceeds, after taxes, would be donated to charity. By 2008, over $280 million had been given to thousands of charities.

One beneficiary of his philanthropy is the Hole in the Wall Gang Camp, a residential summer camp for children with serious illnesses. Newman co-founded the camp in 1988, and named it after the gang in his film *Butch Cassidy and the Sundance Kid*. The camp serves 13,000 children every year, at no cost to the participants.

By the time he died in 2008, Newman had donated significantly more than he earned during his acting career. When asked why, he said, "I'm not running for sainthood. I just happen to think that in life we need to be a little like the farmer, who puts back into the soil what he takes out."

CHAMPION FOR THE DISABLED

Eunice Kennedy Shriver was born into one of the most powerful American dynasties in history. Two of her brothers were U.S. Senators, and another was the 35th President of the United States.

Though she never ran for political office herself, her boundless passion equaled that of her brothers. Inspired by her developmentally disabled sister, Rosemary, Shriver devoted much of her life to helping people with mental disabilities. Her greatest accomplishment was founding the Special Olympics, an organization that sponsors competitions for disabled athletes.

In 1962, Shriver started a summer day camp for developmentally disabled children and adults at her home in Maryland. She wanted to provide a means by which campers could explore their capabilities in a variety of sports and physical activities. The camp quickly expanded, and the first Special Olympics was held in 1968 at Soldier Field in Chicago.

Although Eunice Shriver passed away in 2009, her legacy lives on. Shriver understood the Biblical lesson taught to her by her parents—that much is expected of those to whom much has been given. She responded to that expectation, and worked fervently to end the stigmas associated with mental disabilities.

From a backyard summer camp to a global movement, Special Olympics has been changing lives and attitudes for more than 40 years. Today, the organization serves almost 3 million athletes in 180 countries.

MOBILIZING YOUTH TO CHANGE THE WORLD

Dylan Mahalingam sat at the dinner table, stubbornly refusing to eat the rest of his dinner, because he didn't like what his mother had served. We can all relate to the conversation that followed, when Dylan's parents told him the food he was wasting on his plate was enough to feed a whole family for a week in countries that were less privileged than ours.

Though he was only three years old at the time, Dylan began to wonder how he could get his plate full of food to someone less fortunate than him in a completely different country. His parents' lecture planted a seed—one that would not only change young Dylan's life, but would make a difference in the lives of thousands of people around the world.

If the dinner conversation was the planting, that seed was watered when Dylan was nine years old. His family traveled to India, and Dylan saw up close the poverty that his parents had described. After talking with his older sister, he started Lil' MDGs, a group whose mission is to leverage the power of the Internet to educate, engage, inspire, and empower youth in all corners of the world to work together to meet the United Nations Millennium Development Goals (MDGs). The eight goals of the UN include ending poverty and hunger, universal education, gender equality, and combating AIDS and HIV.

Since it was launched, Lil' MDGs has mobilized children from 31 states and 34 countries to raise $780,000 for tsunami relief in Southeast Asia, and more than $10 million for hurricane relief in areas impacted by Katrina and Rita. But the support didn't stop there. When Dylan turned 10, he used his birthday as a platform to raise money for Tibet's Lamdrak School, asking friends and family to donate money in lieu of presents. The group has also raised money to benefit the Nyaka School in Uganda, and assisted with a fundraiser to fight the genocide raging in Darfur, Sudan.

"What I have discovered," said Dylan, "is that children want to help and get involved, and most of them find it fun, fascinating, rewarding, and less intimidating to use technology to accomplish this. Lil' MDGs is making it possible for them to do both."

Truly Blessed

If you are reading this book, then you can count yourself among the most fortunate people in the world. You have probably eaten a meal or two already today, you will have a roof over your head tonight and, relatively speaking anyway, life is working at least "okay" for you.

What you must realize is that this is not the case for everyone. In fact, we live in a world that is not working for many, many people. Consider the following statistics, which contain the most recent data at the time this book was written:

- There are an estimated 774 million illiterate adults in the world.
- 1.3 billion people live on less than a dollar a day.
- Half the world's population are living on two dollars a day, and 800 million people are malnourished in developing countries.
- 1.3 billion people have no clean water.
- 2 billion people have no sanitation.
- 2 billion people have no electricity.

While we often think of poverty as something that exists far away in third world countries, it also exists in the United States. It exists in each state, and I am guessing that you could find people within 15 or 20 minutes of your house, if not closer, who are struggling to make life work for them.

I believe we are all called to make a difference in the world. Regardless of what we *don't* have, there's a lot that we do have. And we all have within us the ability to positively impact other people. It is our responsibility to answer that call.

The Joy of Giving

If you are a Christian, the Bible is very clear about our responsibility to help others. Here are a few verses that encourage Christ-followers to make a difference:

- Jesus answered, "If you want to be perfect, go, sell your possessions and give to the poor, and you will have treasure in heaven. Then come, follow me." — Matthew 19:21
- For I was hungry and you gave me something to eat, I was thirsty and you gave me something to drink, I was a stranger and you invited me in, I needed clothes and you clothed me, I was sick and you looked after me, I was in prison and you came to visit me. — Matthew 25:35–36
- On the contrary: If your enemy is hungry, feed him; if he is thirsty, give him something to drink . . . — Romans 12:20

- This is how we know what love is: Jesus Christ laid down his life for us. And we ought to lay down our lives for our brothers. If anyone has material possessions and sees his brother in need but has no pity on him, how can the love of God be in him? Dear children, let us not love with words or tongue but with actions and in truth.
  — 1 John 3:16–18

Positively impacting other people isn't a religious issue, though. One of the greatest joys we can experience as human beings, whether you are a Christian or not, is to make a difference in the world. To be generous. To help other people.

> *The happiest people in the world are those who do the most for others.*
> —*Booker T. Washington*

Making a difference provides two benefits. First, those who receive your gifts benefit from your generosity. There are people in need within your own community, and throughout the world. You get to be part of the solution, helping the world to work better for someone other than yourself.

The second benefit is the joy you get to experience by helping other people. As you go the extra mile to make a difference for others, your life will be transformed, as well. Sometimes it's just a feeling you get from knowing that someone benefited from your generosity. That feeling is even stronger when you actually get to see the difference you've made in someone else's life.

Holy Discontent

One of the challenges for many people is figuring out where to start. I think people generally want to help others, but they have a hard time moving from desire into action. Part of this stems from the difficulty of deciding which causes or organizations to support.

Bill Hybels, senior pastor of Willow Creek Community Church in South Barrington, Illinois, offers a great way to discover where you can make a difference. He invites you to answer the following question:

What is the one aspect of this broken world that, when you see it, touch it, get near it, you just can't stand?

In his book, *Holy Discontent: Fueling the Fire That Ignites Personal Vision*, Hybels explains that your answer to that question reveals your "holy discontent," an issue so troubling that you can't stand it. This issue will be different for different people.

We are often paralyzed by the frustration of things that are not working in the world. The problems seem too big for us to make even the slightest difference, let alone solve them. But you *can* do *something*. If you can turn your frustration into motivation to fix what's broken, not only will *your* life be impacted, but you can make a difference for *others*, too.

Here are three well-known examples of people who did just that:

• She lived in the slums of India, had no possessions or money of her own, and shunned material comforts. Yet she accomplished things for the poor that no one else had or likely will. For 60 years, Mother Teresa immersed herself in the world of the impoverished, the uncared for, and the deserted. She lived as they lived, she ate as they ate, she wore what they wore.

> *Let us not be satisfied with just giving money. I would like more people to give their hands to serve and their hearts to love—to recognize the poor . . . to reach out to them in love and compassion.*
>
> —Mother Teresa

In 1950, Mother Teresa petitioned the church to open her own religious order, which she named the Missionaries of Charity. It began with 12 members in Calcutta, India, and would grow to include more than 4,000 nuns and 120,000 volunteers. Together, the organization runs 600 houses for the poor in more than 130 countries, and employs more than a million workers.

• As a college student, Nelson Mandela became increasingly aware of the racial injustice faced by non-white citizens of South Africa. He took an active role in the struggle against apartheid, and was later arrested for treason. He was imprisoned for 26 years.

Mandela's imprisonment was not in vain, however, as it led to worldwide pressure for his release, and for an end to apartheid. In April 1994, four years after his release, his country held its first multi-racial elections, and Nelson Mandela was elected President of South Africa.

• As a young girl, Jane Goodall dreamed of living with animals in Africa. With her mother's encouragement, Goodall went to Africa in 1957, at the age of 23. She lived in the jungles of the Gombe Game Reserve, and would remain there for more than two decades. Goodall's unique method of studying animals in the wild, which empha-

> *The least I can do is speak out for those who cannot speak for themselves.*
>
> *—Jane Goodall*

sized patient observation over long periods of time, led to her becoming the world's foremost authority on chimpanzees.

Goodall expanded her global outreach with the founding of the Jane Goodall Institute for Wildlife Research, Education, and Conservation. Although she no longer lives in Africa, Goodall continues her mission by lecturing, writing, and encouraging the appreciation of chimpanzees and other primates.

Mother Teresa dreamed of a world where the poor and helpless are cared for, and people reach out to others with love and compassion.

Nelson Mandela dreamed of a world where apartheid is abolished, and the ethnic divide between blacks and whites no longer exists.

Jane Goodall dreamed of a world where chimpanzees and their habitat are protected, and the interdependence between man and everything in nature is respected.

> *You must be the change you wish to see in the world.*
>
> —*Mohandas Gandhi*

What about you? What is the one aspect of this broken world that, when you see it, touch it, get near it, you just can't stand? Determine your "holy discontent," then channel your frustration into effective action. Decide today how you will positively impact others, and make a difference in the world.

Ways to Give

Once you've determined *where* you're going to make a difference, the next step is to determine *how* you will help others. For this, I recommend reviewing your time, talents, and treasures.

How wonderful it is that nobody need wait a single moment before starting to improve the world.
—Anne Frank

The "three Ts" might seem a bit cliché when talking about contribution. But this structure for giving has been around for a very long time. Indeed, it's based in Scripture, and a considerable amount of attention is devoted to this topic in the Bible. These methods of contribution also reflect the true needs of individuals and organizations, and the gifts we can provide to help them.

At different times in your life, you will be positioned differently in terms of your ability to positively impact organizations. Ideally, you would contribute all three Ts. Sometimes, however, life gets in the way. You might have more time than money at a certain stage in your life, or have more money than time at another stage.

Here are a few specific ways you might share your time, talents, and treasures:

- *Time*

Giving your time to people and organizations in need is at least as important as giving money. Without the countless hours of service from selfless volunteers, many organizations simply could not function.

There are many ways to give of your time. You can work at the local soup kitchen. You can visit the elderly at a nursing home. There are a variety of service opportunities in your church. You could mentor a boy or girl, and share some of the lessons contained in this book.

Another very important use of your time is to pray. Always include those who are less fortunate than you in your prayers. Pray for the poor. Pray for those who are sick. Pray for the lost. As you serve in various organizations, pray for specific people with whom you come into contact.

• *Talents*

The first part of contributing your talents is identifying where your talents lie, and determining how they can best be used for the service of others.

What gifts do you have to offer that you can share? If you are gifted with musical ability, then you could sing in the choir, or play in the band at church. You could also participate in community organizations, such as the local symphony. If you have accounting, legal, or administrative skills, non-profit organizations are always looking for people with those gifts. If you possess technical expertise, such as plumbing or carpentry, you could help an organization such as Habitat for Humanity. Organizations, or even your elderly neighbor, can always use help with such tasks as mowing the lawn in the summer, or planting flowers in the spring.

Everyone has talents, and opportunities exist for every talent to be used in serving others. What are your talents, and how can you share in a way that benefits others?

• *Treasures*

One of the greatest blessings I've received in life is the gift of contributing financially to people and organizations in need. The mistake many people make is thinking that contributing money will cause them to have *less*. Looking at things from a very narrow perspective, it does cause you to have less money than you had before the contribution.

In the bigger picture, however, we gain far more by contributing financially. Accept this on faith for now,

> *When you give, you always end up with more. Sometimes more in your hands. Always more in your heart.*
>
> —Dave Ramsey

until you can experience this powerful blessing for yourself. Make financial giving a part of your commitment to make a difference in the world.

Think Big but Act Small

I think people generally want to help others, but they have a hard time moving from desire into action. Part of this revolves around the belief that, in order to make an impact on society, they must do something huge.

The stories in this chapter have probably perpetuated that belief. They illustrate people who have changed the world in dramatic ways through their contribution. One thing to remember, though, is each person cited was an ordinary person—just like you and me—who ended up doing extraordinary things. Just as they had the ability to impact change in the world, so do you.

You might think that the small actions you are capable of won't really make a difference. The truth is, your small gestures, when repeated over time, will make a huge impact on society. This works very much like the concept of compound interest discussed in Chapter 7.

Just consider the following people, all of whom have been nominated as *CNN Everyday Heroes*:

- Irene Zola matches volunteers with the elderly in her New York City neighborhood to help with their day-to-day needs. All of the seniors and most of the volunteers live within the same 24-block radius.
- Texas homebuilder Dan Wallrath provides mortgage-free homes for injured veterans through his foundation, *Operation Finally Home.*
- Susan Burton of Los Angeles developed a non-profit that provides housing and support to formerly incarcerated women.

There are so many people throughout this country and the world whose small gestures are making a difference for the people and organizations they serve. Instead of worrying about the immediate size of your contribution, take a baby step—any baby step.

> *If you can't feed a hundred people, then feed just one.*
>
> —*Mother Teresa*

Instead of focusing on what you *can't* do, focus on what you *can* do. Instead of focusing on what you *don't* have, focus on what you *do* have. Think big, but act small. Start today, wherever you are.

Commit to Serving Others

A few months ago, I received an email containing a quiz that was designed to make you think about life. Unlike many of the emails that I quickly delete, I saved this one. It's a perfect illustration of the impact we can have on others by making a difference.

Go ahead and take the quiz yourself, and you'll see what I mean:

1. Name the five wealthiest people in the world.
2. Name the last three winners of the Super Bowl, and the MVPs of each team.
3. Name the last three winners of the Miss America contest.

4. Name ten people who have won the Nobel Peace Prize.
5. Name the last three Academy Award winners for Best Actor and Best Actress.

How did you do? The point is, we don't remember those who made the headlines of the Sunday paper, *ESPN SportsCenter's* Top 10, or the covers of *People* magazine. These accolades are truly impressive, and are earned by people who are the best in their field. But the applause dies. Awards tarnish. Their achievements are soon forgotten.

Here's another quiz. See how you do on this one:

1. Name the three teachers who impacted you the most in school.
2. Name three friends who were there when you needed them.
3. Name three people who made you feel appreciated and special.
4. Name five people you enjoy spending time with.
5. Name three heroes whose stories have inspired you the most.

The lesson? The people who make a difference in your life are not the ones with the most money, talent, or awards. They are the ones who care.

In his book, *Living a Life That Matters*, Rabbi Harold Kushner writes about his experience tending to people in the last moments of their lives. What he found was the people who had the most difficult time with death were those who felt they hadn't done anything worthwhile with their lives. "It was not the death that frightened them," Kushner wrote, "It was insignificance, the fear that they would die and leave no mark on the world."

The good news is you still have plenty of time to do worthwhile things with your life. If you're young, then make the commitment to serve others. If you're in the later years of your life, there is still time to positively impact other people. In fact, you can start making a difference today!

> *Never doubt that a small group of committed citizens can change the world. Indeed, it is the only thing that ever has.*
> —Margaret Mead

Be the kind of person that cares. Make the choice to impact everyone you come in contact with in a positive way. You have the power to make a difference in people's lives, and therefore to make a difference in the world.

What I want for you is that—one year, five years, or twenty years from now—someone is writing your name when they take that quiz. Make a difference . . . starting today!

LIFE LESSONS

✓ What is your "holy discontent"—the one aspect of this broken world that, when you see it, touch it, get near it, you just can't stand? Take out a sheet of paper, and write about your frustration around this issue.

✓ Review your time, talents, and treasures. How specifically can you share your gifts in a way that will benefit others?

✓ Imagine yourself five years into the future. Looking back on the impact you've made, what have you done during those five years to help other people, and to make a difference in the world? Create a plan to make that difference, and do *something*—starting today—to make that plan a reality.

✓ Resolve to perform one "random act of kindness" every day. Allow the person behind you at the grocery store to go ahead of you when he only has one or two items. Have lunch delivered for you and your co-workers, and pick up the tab. Send a note of appreciation to someone who has made a positive impact on your life. Do something simple every day to show that you care.

The Starfish Story

(Inspired by Loren Eisley's "The Star Thrower")

One day a man was walking along the beach when he noticed a boy picking something up and gently throwing it into the ocean.

Approaching the boy, he asked, "What are you doing?"

The youth replied, "Throwing starfish into the ocean. The surf is up and the tide is going out. If I don't throw them back, they'll die."

"Son," the man said, "don't you realize there are miles and miles of beach and hundreds of starfish? You can't possibly make a difference!"

After listening politely for a moment, the boy bent down, picked up another starfish, and threw it back into the sea. Smiling at the man, he said, "I made a difference for that one."

"I spent years on the Road to Success,
but I was driving in the wrong direction!"

CHAPTER 13

LEARN TO BE HAPPY WITH WHAT YOU HAVE

I know what it is to be in need, and I know what it is to have plenty. I have learned the secret of being content in any and every situation, whether well fed or hungry, whether living in plenty or in want.
—PHILIPPIANS 4:12

COUNT YOUR BLESSINGS

If you woke up this morning with more health than illness . . . you are more blessed than the million who will not survive this week.

If you have never experienced the danger of battle, the loneliness of imprisonment, the agony of torture, or the pangs of starvation . . . you are ahead of 500 million people in the world.

If you can attend a religious or political meeting without fear of harassment, arrest, torture, or death . . . you are more blessed than three billion people in the world.

If you have food in the refrigerator, clothes on your back, a roof overhead, and a place to sleep . . . you are richer than 75% of this world.

If you have money in the bank, in your wallet, and spare change in a dish someplace . . . you are among the top 8% of the world's wealthy.

If your parents are still alive and still married . . . you are very rare, even in the United States.

If you can hold up your head with a smile on your face and are truly thankful . . . you are blessed because the majority can, but most do not.

A MATTER OF PERSPECTIVE

The wealthy CEO of a large organization decided that it was time to show his son a little more of the world. In particular, he wanted to make sure his son understood how much he had to be grateful for. So he made arrangements for the two of them to visit a very poor family in the country.

On the ride back in the car, the father asked what the son learned from the trip.

"Well, Dad," said the son, "I never realized until now just how poor we were."

The father was speechless. After all, the whole point of the trip was to show his son how much he had to be grateful for. Afraid that his son had missed the point entirely, he asked him to explain.

"Well, their land goes on forever, while we have only a small parcel," said the boy. "Their yard is lit by the stars, while ours is lit by fancy lanterns. They swim in a creek that goes on for miles, while we are confined to an Olympic-sized pool. They grow their own food, while we have to go to the grocery store to buy ours. They are always helping others, while we have servants."

> It is not the man who has little, but he who desires more, that is poor.
> —*Seneca*

The father sat for a moment, in silence. Then he said, "I brought you on this trip to teach you something, and you taught me something instead. You have shown me that poverty is a matter of perspective. Thank you for teaching me that it's not the material things we have that determine whether we are fortunate."

PLAIN ICE CREAM

In the days when an ice cream sundae cost much less than it does now, a 10-year-old boy entered a restaurant and sat down at the table. When the waitress greeted him, he asked, "How much is an ice cream sundae?"

"Fifty cents," replied the waitress. The little boy pulled a handful of coins out of his pocket, and studied them for a moment. "Well," he continued, "how much for plain ice cream?" The waitress was growing impatient, as other customers were now lined up, waiting to be seated. "Thirty-five cents," she responded. The little boy counted his coins again, then said "May I please have the plain ice cream?"

> *You can't always get what you want. But if you try sometime, you might find you get what you need.*
>
> —*Mick Jagger*

Moments later, the waitress brought the vanilla ice cream. She ripped the bill from her order pad, placed in on the table next to the ice cream, and walked away. The boy quietly ate his ice cream, paid the cashier, and left.

A few minutes later, the waitress returned to the table to wipe it down. After pausing for a moment, tears began to roll down her cheeks. On the table, placed neatly beside the empty dish, were a dime and five pennies. The little boy couldn't afford to get the ice cream sundae, because he needed enough money to tip the waitress.

The Paradox of Affluence

We live in a world where we have more affluence than ever before, and yet most people are less satisfied than ever before. Our culture has caused people to continually want more, regardless of how much they already have. The media perpetuates these unrealistic desires, with its constant "give me more" messaging.

Unfortunately, this is a no-win situation. As long as we continue to desire the latest and greatest cell phones, computers, cars, and clothes, we will never be able to satiate our desires. As long as we perceive there's something better around the next corner, we can never be happy with what we already have.

> *The trouble with the rat race is that even if you win, you're still a rat.*
> —Lily Tomlin

There's nothing wrong with having things, or even *wanting* to have them. In fact, much of this book is dedicated to ideas like dreaming big, pursuing goals, and achieving success. While each of those ideas can be applied to relationships, health, spirituality, and other non-material areas, they are also meant to be applied to material goals—earning as much as you can in your job or career, maximizing profits in your business, providing a nice home for your family, and enjoying entertainment and vacations with your loved ones.

For Christians, interpretation of this topic in the Bible sometimes creates confusion. Many people subscribe to the notion that "money is the root of all evil." In fact, that's not what the Bible says. Rather—and this is an important distinction—it states, "For the *love* of money is the root of all kinds of evil."

While it is true that the Bible says "it is harder for a rich man to enter the kingdom of heaven," it is not impossible. We are blessed in so many ways by our Creator, and for some people that blessing has manifested itself through economic abundance. I believe God wants His people to be "successful" in every area of their lives, including the area of money and material possessions.

> *The root to abundance is through the doorway of enough.*
>
> —*Lynne Twist*

One question to ask yourself is, "Where is my focus?" Is it on buying the next "thing," or on pursuing financial independence to the detriment of other (arguably more important) areas of your life? Or is it on being the best you can be, in *every* area of your life, which includes providing the best life you can for you and your family?

Another question to examine is, "Where is my heart?" Is it rooted in greed for more stuff, envy when your friend or neighbor has something that you don't, or lusting after the material trappings of the world?

Or is your heart with God first, your family next, and everything else after that?

Television, the advertising industry, and today's popular culture make it very difficult to keep priorities in the right order. But it *is* possible to do so. For me, the distinction is found in this phrase:

"Learn to be happy with what you have, while you pursue all you want."

Most people have no trouble whatsoever with the latter part of that phrase. They know how to "pursue" the things they want. But once they have what they've so tirelessly pursued, they don't know how to be happy with it. They become caught up in the notion that there's still something better out there.

So how do you break this cycle? Well, like any change, a change of attitude is best achieved with lots of practice. If you make a conscious effort to be happy and content, your efforts will turn into a habit.

Studies suggest that the way you act significantly affects the way you feel. People who *act* confident in a job interview, even if they feel insecure inside, end up *feeling* confident. People who smile eventually end up feeling happy. The same thing goes for gratitude. If you *act* grateful and content, eventually you'll *feel* grateful and content.

In her book, *The How of Happiness: A Scientific Approach to Getting the Life You Want*, research psychologist and

University of California professor of Psychology, Sonja Lyubomirsky, describes more than a dozen uniquely formulated strategies to increase happiness. What's her Happiness Activity #1? Expressing gratitude.

Consciously Express Gratitude

The first step in learning to be happy with what you have is to consciously express gratitude. Starting today, make an effort to do the following things:

• **Catch people doing things well.** Most people are quick to notice inferiority—when our kids don't get the grades we expect, when someone at work isn't performing up to expectations, when service in a restaurant is below what we expect. You may have even gone out of your way to point out the poor service to a restaurant manager, or the customer service representative of an organization whose product or service did not meet your expectations. But how often do you call a customer service representative out of the blue to tell them how *good* their product or service is?

Most people aren't as quick to catch people exceeding expectations. And even if they notice it, they tend not to praise superior behavior. Whether we realize it or not, this has serious ramifications for our society. For example, in a survey cited by *Fast Company* magazine, in which

10,000 employees from the 1,000 largest companies were interviewed, 40% of workers cited "lack of recognition" as the primary reason for leaving a job.

Starting today, make a point of "catching" people exceeding expectations—and praise them for doing so. Instead of complaining about your flight being delayed, praise the actions of the crew that served you during the flight, and delivered you safely to your destination. Whenever you feel like complaining about something, look for something to be grateful for instead.

• **Make "thank you" a regular part of your life.** "Thank you" is such a simple phrase—two little words—yet it's one we often forget. It's so easy to say, and it can have a wonderfully positive impact on the recipient. Incorporate the words "thank you" into your vocabulary, and into your life.

One way to make "thank you" a regular part of your life is by sending thank you notes—for everything. I believe writing thank you notes is so important that it's one of the *Success Habits* in Chapter 6.

It's an absolute "must" to send a thank you note whenever you receive a gift from someone. Go above and beyond, though, and send a note for reasons that are less obvious, and maybe even unexpected. It only takes a few minutes, but the effect lasts a long time.

For example, after enjoying lunch with a friend, acquaintance, or colleague you haven't seen in a while, send them a note after to "thank" them for their time and friendship. Even if *you* picked up the tab. Your note will send a message that they are appreciated.

Another opportunity to express appreciation is when an employee of a company has helped you in a way that stands out as being "above and beyond the call of duty." This will have a positive impact not only on the employee, but also on management, who is accustomed to receiving only complaints, not praise.

> *Of all the "attitudes" we can acquire, surely the attitude of gratitude is the most important and by far the most life changing.*
>
> —Zig Ziglar

Recently, during a trip to Las Vegas, I stayed at the Wynn Hotel. When I left, I checked out without receiving the hotel bill. A couple of days later I called to get the bill, and I spoke with a very helpful accounts receivable clerk named Kate, who promised to email it to me right away.

Well, I never received the bill. I called Kate back, and she agreed to fax it to me. As luck would have it, my fax machine was on the fritz. I had to call back and request the bill *yet again*—a third time. This was getting silly!

Technological difficulties prevented me from receiving this bill, and it would have been very easy to become frustrated. You know how it goes—something goes wrong so you blame the customer service person. He or she loses patience and becomes less friendly and eager to help. Negativity abounds. We've all been there.

In this case, however, Kate remained pleasant and dedicated to seeing that my request was fulfilled. It was crazy that so many attempts had to be made to get this bill, but I recognized and appreciated Kate's willingness to help. I told her I would "put in a good word for her with Steve (Wynn, the owner of the hotel)." She chuckled in a way that indicated she might not believe me. After all, this had been somewhat of a nightmare scenario. I meant what I said, though, and I sent Mr. Wynn a note praising the way Kate handled the situation.

• **Write gratitude letters.** If you really want to take "thank you" to the next level, then writing letters of gratitude is the way to go. Make a list of all the people who have made a difference in your life—the teacher who instilled in you the love of reading, the coach whose belief in you helped you achieve the next level, the friend who gave you some advice that changed your life.

Once a week or so, write a letter to someone on your list. Thank that person for the specific reason they are on your list. Then mail or deliver the letter. Your expression of gratitude will be appreciated by the recipient, and it will make you feel pretty good, too.

• **Keep a "gratitude journal."** This can be a fancy hardcover book, or a simple spiral-bound notebook. Commit to a regular writing time—either once a day or once a week—and write down three to five things that you are grateful for.

> *Wealth consists not in having great possessions but in having few wants.*
>
> —*Esther de Waal*

Keeping a gratitude journal only takes a couple of minutes, but it will give you a tremendous boost of happiness and joy. Try it, and notice how your gratitude for the blessings in life is enhanced!

As the Chinese philosopher Lao Tzu wrote more than 2,000 years ago:

> "If you look to others for fulfillment, you will never truly be fulfilled.
> If your happiness depends on money, you will never be happy with yourself.
> Be content with what you have; rejoice in the way things are.
> When you realize there is nothing lacking, the whole world belongs to you."

Make the decision right now to thoroughly enjoy all that you have been blessed with. Be grateful, and express that gratitude regularly. With that mindset, continue to pursue the mighty blessings that God still has planned for you. You deserve it, and that is God's gift to you.

LIFE LESSONS

✓ Re-read the stories at the beginning of this chapter. Think about how blessed you are, and make a list of at least three non-material things for which you are grateful.

✓ Resolve today to consciously express gratitude on an ongoing basis. Catch people exceeding expectations, and praise them for doing so.

✓ Whenever you feel like complaining, resist the temptation to do so. Find something about the situation to be grateful for instead.

For inspirational stories about gratitude and other topics discussed in *Life Lessons*, go to:

www.lifelessonsthebook.com/blog.

CHAPTER 14

MAKE EACH DAY YOUR MASTERPIECE

*Twenty years from now you will be more
disappointed by the things you didn't do than by
the ones you did do. So throw off the bowlines.
Sail away from the safe harbor. Catch the trade
winds in your sails. Explore. Dream. Discover.*

—MARK TWAIN

THE LAST LECTURE

What would you do if you were 47 years old, dying of pancreatic cancer, and knew you only had a few months to live?

If you were Carnegie Mellon professor Dr. Randy Pausch, you'd give one last lecture before you stepped down from academic duties to spend the remaining days of your life with your family.

Pausch's lecture was not about computer science, a subject that he had taught for 20 years. Nor was it about cancer, which he found out about a year before the lecture. In an effort to impart as much wisdom as possible to his three young children, Pausch's final talk was about achieving your childhood dreams.

Some of Pausch's advice? Imagine. Tell the truth. Show gratitude. Believe that no job is beneath you. Draw on the walls.

"I don't know how to not have fun," he said in his lecture, which was eventually turned into a bestselling book called *The Last Lecture*. "I'm dying and I'm having fun. And I'm going to keep having fun every day I have left. Because there's no other way to play it. . . . Pretty much any time I got a chance to do something cool I tried to grab for it, and that's where my solace comes from."

High Aspirations

Since boyhood, Australian mountain climber Mark Inglis dreamed of standing on the top of Mount Everest. That dream was jeopardized in 1982, however, when a climbing mishap left him stranded in an ice cave for 14 days. Inglis lost both legs below the knee to frostbite.

Instead of lamenting the loss of his legs, Inglis turned stumbling blocks into stepping-stones. He became a world-class international skier in the 1990s, and won a silver medal on the cycling track in the 2000 Paralympics. In 2002, he decided it was time to head back up the mountains, and summited Aoraki/ Mount Cook, the highest

> *Shoot for the moon.*
> *Even if you miss, you'll*
> *land among the stars.*
> —*Author unknown*

mountain in New Zealand. On his 45th birthday in 2004, he ascended Cho Oyu in Nepal, the 6th highest mountain in the world. In doing so, Inglis became only the second amputee to ascend an 8,000-meter peak.

For most people, that would have been enough. But Inglis had never lost sight of his childhood dream. On May 15, 2006, he became the first double amputee to stand on the summit of Mount Everest. In the process he raised tens of thousands of dollars for the Cambodia Trust, which furnishes prosthetic devices to amputees, and offers support to help people with disabilities achieve their full potential.

WINNING AT LIFE

Legendary basketball coach John Wooden is the most successful coach in history. His accomplishments at UCLA include winning ten NCAA national championships, including seven in a row from 1967 to 1973, and four perfect 30–0 seasons.

But what few people realize is that Wooden was a model of success not only in basketball, but also in life. Wooden's non-basketball honors include being named California "Sports Father of the Year" and receiving the Presidential Medal of Freedom, the nation's highest civilian honor.

Several traits contributed to his success both on and off the court, and Wooden's success philosophy is documented in his famous "Pyramid of Success." But the one that stands out more than any other is the advice given to him by his father when Wooden graduated from grammar school: *Make each day your masterpiece.*

Wooden understood that you can't change the past, and that you shouldn't live in the future, either. While you can certainly learn from the past, and you can definitely do things now that will affect the future, Wooden knew that life was happening right now. He focused on today, both in his personal life and as a coach. Wooden wanted to end each day thinking that he had done his best. And he instilled this philosophy in his players.

Going Through the Motions

Have you ever noticed how some people are stuck going through the motions of life? Their routine consists of waking up, going to work, coming home, eating, and going to bed. Maybe they eat at a restaurant once or twice a month, or catch a movie here and there. But for the most part, their lives become caught in routine, everyday living.

> *How different our lives are when we really know what is deeply important to us and, keeping that picture in mind, we manage ourselves each day to be and to do what really matters most.*
>
> —*Stephen R. Covey*

The danger in "going through the motions" is that things that really matter have the tendency to fall by the wayside. We forget to live in the moment. To continue Coach Wooden's basketball metaphor, instead of living each day as if it's a championship game, people live as though it's a practice for some game in the future.

How does this manifest itself? Well, instead of savoring life, we tend to "save" it. We wait until things are "lined up" just right.

- We "save" our most prized possessions and wait for a "special occasion" to use them. But then that special occasion never comes, and so we never end up using the things we worked so hard to obtain. Instead, our potential experiences sit on a shelf, hang on a hook, or languish in a drawer.

- We "save" our emotions and feelings. We don't tell people how we feel about them, because we think we have time. But what if we don't? God doesn't promise us tomorrow. Perhaps you've already attended a funeral and thought, "I wish I had told Grandma how much I loved her," or "I wish I had told my sister I was sorry."

- We "save" our plans for a better time. We put our dreams on hold for "later"—for a better time with better circumstances. But that "perfect" time never really comes, and life marches on.

Living Life to the Fullest

If you think about it for a minute, you probably know how you're doing in this area. If it's not something you've given much thought to, simply answer these four questions:

1. Are you living life to the fullest?
2. What would you do differently if you knew you only had one year to live?

3. What if you knew you had just one week to live?
4. What would you do differently if you knew that today was your *last* day on earth?

I ask these questions not to be morbid or negative, or to dwell on issues you'd rather not contemplate. I ask them because you have the wonderful opportunity to think about "how you would live your life if . . ." and to begin living that life today. You have the opportunity to make adjustments in the way

> *Five hundred twenty-five thousand six hundred minutes, how do you measure, measure a year?*
>
> —Lyrics from Seasons of Love, *from the musical* Rent

you live your life—to position yourself so you are doing the things that are important—in order to make each day a "masterpiece."

If you're reading this, then you're probably not lying on your deathbed, longing for another chance. People who have come close to death often say that they have different priorities than they did before. They don't take things for granted anymore. They realize how short life is, and how quickly it can end. Their focus changes.

None of them, when reflecting in their hospital bed, think, "If I make it through this, I'm going to spend more time at work." Rather, they think about doing more of what they love to do. They think about enjoying more time with their family. They think about the difference they can make—in their own lives, and in the lives of others.

Don't wait until you're lying on your deathbed. Don't wait until tragedy strikes someone around you. Live life *now*. Make each day your masterpiece.

> *Life is either a daring adventure or nothing.*
> —*Helen Keller*

Here's the good news: Whether you're a child, or a teenager, or an adult, today is the first day of the rest of your life. You get to choose to live your best life. Here are some questions to think about that will help you make each day a masterpiece:

- **What kind of person do you want to be?** Do you want to listen more and talk less? Do you want to smile more? Worry less? Be more relaxed, with less stress? Do you want to be more spontaneous, to have more fun? Do you want to be more curious?

- **What do you want to be doing?** Do you want to read more and watch less TV? Visit museums more and Blockbuster less? Do you want to listen to more classical music? Learn a hobby, or a foreign language? Do you want to enroll in an aerobics class, or learn yoga? Do you want to eat more fruit, and fewer french fries?

- **What kind of parent/child/friend do you want to be?** Do you want to hug more, and yell less? Do you want to keep in touch with friends, especially the ones who have moved away? Do you want to, just once, eat spaghetti on the living room floor? Let the kids draw on the walls? Get grass stains on your new pants? Do you want to say, "I know it's getting late and you have school tomorrow, but let's read just one more chapter"? Do you want to go for more bike rides? Fly more kites? Have more meaningful conversations with friends and family members? Do you want to say more "I love you's," more "I'm sorry's," and more "thank you's"?

> *Life is not measured by the number of breaths we take, but by the moments that take our breath away.*
>
> —*Author unknown*

- **What can you do, starting today, that will matter 100 years from now?** While it's important to live for today, it's also important to live for something bigger than yourself. Most of what we do in our lives will not be remembered 100 years from now. What can you do that *will* matter?

At the beginning of each day, ask yourself, "What is the single most important thing I can do today to make my life a masterpiece?" At the end of the day, ask yourself,

"How did I do? What worked, and what didn't work? What will I change tomorrow?"

Decide what kind of person you want to be, and start living that way. Dr. Martin Luther King Jr. once said, "Not everyone can be famous, but *everyone* can be great." Choose to be great—today, and every day. Embrace life as it happens. Live life *now*, and make each day your masterpiece!

LIFE LESSONS

✓ Make a list of all the things you would do if you found out you only had one year to live. Commit to doing at least some of them in the next 12 months. Take action this week toward the one you're going to do first.

✓ Go through your house and gather any possessions that you have been "saving" for a special occasion. Make plans to use them this week.

✓ Call a friend you haven't talked to in a while. Tell someone in your family that you love them. Give yourself permission to do something you've been putting off.

✓ Resolve today that you are going to leave a legacy for future generations. Determine what you can do that will matter 100 years from now. Set it as a goal, make plans to achieve it, and begin working on your plan immediately.

What have you done to make your day a "masterpiece?" Share your comments at:

www.lifelessonsthebook.com

SECTION II
FINAL THOUGHTS

How Will You Fill Your Blank Page?

As I begin this last page—my final words of wisdom regarding the important lessons I want you to know—I am reminded of a school experience when I was asked to "take out a blank sheet of paper." I did so, without knowing the assignment that would soon be given. I was asked to write an essay about a given topic. By the time I finished, that blank sheet of paper was filled.

And now, so it is with your life. I want you to imagine a blank page representing the next chapter in your life. Your "assignment" is to fill in the blank sheet of paper, the canvas of your life. How you fill this blank page represents how you will live your life, and the imprint you will make on the world.

Think about the difference you can make today, tomorrow, and in the next few years of your life. You will meet new people along the way, and you will have opportunities to make a difference in their lives. What impact will you have on them? What impact will you make in your family? How will you make a difference in your career? How, by the time your life is over, will the world have been positively impacted because of the contributions you made to it?

Dream big, and believe in your ability to impact the world in small ways, and in big ways. Be optimistic about the future, and about your role in it.

I commend you for making it through the book, and I look forward with eager anticipation to seeing how you will fill your blank page. Send me a note or an email, and let me know how you're doing on your journey. I would love to hear from you!

BRIAN BARTES
PO Box 700424 • Plymouth, MI 48170
brian@lifeexcellence.com • www.lifelessonsthebook.com

SECTION III
RESOURCES

FREE GIFT!

As a token of my appreciation for reading this book, I would like to send you a free *Life Lessons* coffee mug. All you need to do is send five personal letters, faxes, or emails to people who know and respect you, recommending they buy and read this book. (A sample letter appears on the following page for your convenience.) Then, send me copies of the five letters, along with your own comments about this book. I'll send you a coffee mug as a gift. Send everything to Brian Bartes, c/o Life Lessons Coffee Mug, PO Box 700424, Plymouth, Michigan 48170. Sorry, but the offer expires December 31, 2012.

Sample Letter

From: _____

Dear: _____:

I just finished one of the BEST books on success I have ever read, and I thought you would want to know about it. It's a great book for anyone who wants to improve his or her life. It's going to change my life in a positive way, and I bet you'll want to read it, too.

The book is called *Life Lessons: A Guide to Creating and Living Your Best Life*, by Brian Bartes. You can order it directly from the Life Lessons website, at *www.lifelessonsthebook.com*.

You can thank me later. Get the book now!!

Sincerely,

_____

Suggested Reading

The Bible.

Alcorn, Randy. *The Treasury Principle.*

Allen, James. *As a Man Thinketh.*

Canfield, Jack, Mark Victor Hansen and Les Hewitt. *The Power of Focus.*

Carnegie, Dale. *How to Win Friends and Influence People.*

Clason, George S. *The Richest Man in Babylon.*

Conwell, Russell H. *Acres of Diamonds.*

Covey, Stephen R. *The 7 Habits of Highly Effective People.*

Covey, Stephen R., A. Roger Merrill and Rebecca R. Merrill. *First Things First.*

Frankl, Viktor E. *Man's Search for Meaning.*

Hill, Napolean. *Think and Grow Rich.*

Kiyosaki, Robert. *The Cash Flow Quadrant.*

Nightingale, Earl. *The Strangest Secret.*

Pausch, Randy. *The Last Lecture.*

Peale, Norman Vincent. *The Power of Positive Thinking.*

Ramsey, Dave. *Financial Peace Revisited.*

Robbins, Anthony. *Awaken the Giant Within.*

Schwartz, David J. *The Magic of Thinking Big.*

Tracy, Brian. *Focal Point.*

Tracy, Brian. *Maximum Achievement.*

Ziglar, Zig. *See You at the Top.*

ABOUT THE AUTHOR

When asked about his own success, Brian Bartes quickly credits his own application of the *Life Lessons*. As a lifelong student of success and personal development, he reads several books per month, attends seminars and workshops, and is constantly on the lookout for people who are living a great life. For almost 30 years, Brian has observed the common characteristics of happy, successful people, and applied them to his own life.

This strategy has served him well. At the age of 23, Brian became the chief financial officer of a $100 million company, and helped grow it to almost $1 billion in annual revenue. He has also owned several small businesses, including a real estate investment firm and a specialty publishing company. Brian leverages his experience in both large and small businesses to coach and advise small business owners, self-employed professionals, executives, and others to achieve extraordinary results in their personal and professional lives.

Brian constantly strives to grow personally, and to make a positive impact on other people. He actively supports numerous non-profit organizations, and currently serves on the board of Junior Achievement of Southeastern Michigan.

Brian also finds plenty of time for family and fun. He enjoys running, scuba diving, traveling, and collecting sports memorabilia. Brian lives in Plymouth, Michigan with his wife, Heidi, and their four children.

Values List

What is most important in your life? What are the key organizing principles of your life?

Use this list in conjunction with the *Life Lessons* exercises at the end of Chapter 4. After you've written down the positive adjectives that describe the personality and character you aspire to have, review the list below to see if any other values apply. Then, complete the remainder of the exercises.

Abundance
Acceptance
Accomplishment
Accuracy
Achievement
Acknowledgement
Adaptability
Adventure
Affection
Affluence
Aggressiveness
Agility
Alertness
Ambition
Amusement
Anticipation
Appreciation
Assertiveness
Attentiveness
Attractiveness
Awareness
Balance
Beauty
Belonging
Benevolence
Blissfulness
Boldness
Bravery
Brilliance
Calmness
Candor
Capability
Carefulness

Caring
Certainty
Challenge
Cheerfulness
Clarity
Comfort
Commitment
Compassion
Competence
Confidence
Congruency
Connection
Consistency
Contentment
Contribution
Control
Courage
Courtesy
Creativity
Credibility
Curiosity
Daring
Decisiveness
Delight
Dependability
Depth
Desire
Determination
Devotion
Dignity
Diligence
Discipline
Discovery

Discretion

Diversity

Drive

Duty

Eagerness

Education

Effectiveness

Efficiency

Elation

Elegance

Empathy

Encouragement

Endurance

Energy

Enjoyment

Enthusiasm

Excellence

Excitement

Experience

Expertise

Exploration

Expressiveness

Fairness

Faith

Fame

Family

Fidelity

Financial independence

Fitness

Flexibility

Flow

Freedom

Friendliness

Frugality

Fun

Generosity

Giving

Grace

Gratitude

Gregariousness

Growth

Happiness

Harmony

Health

Helpfulness

Honesty

Honor

Hopefulness

Hospitality

Humility

Humor

Imagination

Independence

Insightfulness

Inspiration

Integrity

Intelligence

Intimacy

Intuitiveness

Inventiveness

Investing

Joy

Justice

Kindness

Knowledge

Leadership

Learning
Liberty
Logic
Longevity
Love
Loyalty
Making a difference
Mastery
Modesty
Motivation
Openness
Optimism
Order
Organization
Originality
Passion
Peace
Perceptiveness
Perfection
Perseverance
Persistence
Personal growth
Persuasiveness
Philanthropy
Pleasure
Poise
Positive attitude
Power
Practicality
Precision
Preparedness
Presence
Professionalism

Prosperity
Punctuality
Recognition
Recreation
Reliability
Religion
Resourcefulness
Respect
Risk-taking
Romance
Safety
Security
Service
Significance
Simplicity
Sincerity
Skill
Solitude
Speed
Spirituality
Spontaneity
Stability
Strength
Success
Sympathy
Trust
Truth
Uniqueness
Variety
Virtue
Wealth
Wisdom
Zeal

You can contact Brian Bartes at:

Brian Bartes
PO Box 700424
Plymouth, MI 48170
(734) 254-9970
brian@lifeexcellence.com

If you would like to set up a speaking engagement for Brian Bartes, please contact him at the above number, or via email.

Brian Bartes works with a very limited number of coaching clients. To inquire about coaching opportunities with Brian, please contact him directly at the above number or email address.

FOR ADDITIONAL COPIES OF

LIFE LESSONS
A GUIDE TO CREATING AND LIVING YOUR BEST LIFE

www.lifelessonsthebook.com

Quantity Discounts Available

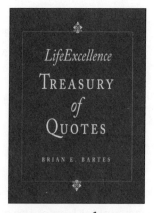

www.treasuryofquotes.com

British politician, novelist and essayist Benjamin Disraeli wrote, "The wisdom of the wise and the experience of the ages are perpetuated by quotations."

LifeExcellence Treasury of Quotes condenses into one small book a lifetime of such wisdom. The quotes contained in this anthology will cause you to reflect and ponder their powerful messages. Some, according to Brian Bartes, will have such an impact that you will be inspired to act, to do something that will make a positive impact in the world.

Short enough to be read in one sitting, the 128-page *LifeExcellence Treasury of Quotes* is a place to visit again and again . . . whenever you need a little inspiration.

This deluxe hardcover edition contains a gold foil stamped Kivar simulated leather case and Smythe sewn binding, with a custom-designed gold foil stamped dust jacket. The elegant, old-world craftsmanship makes *LifeExcellence Treasury of Quotes* the perfect heirloom gift for anyone who appreciates the wisdom of quotes.

Praise for

LifeExcellence
TREASURY OF QUOTES

I love that I have a book that I can go to and find a quote to lift someone's spirit, motivate, or help make a positive impact on someone's life. *LifeExcellence Treasury of Quotes* is a treasury of motivation!

— PATTY LAURENCE, CANTON, MI

This book is an inspirational collection of wisdom. The words are like quiet whispers, and reading this book felt like "coming home."

— MICHELE DEFILIPPO, PHOENIX, AZ

Each quote in Brian's book provides an opportunity for unique reflection and inspiration.

— ALLYSON AABRAM, SAN DIEGO, CA

For more information, or to order
LifeExcellence Treasury of Quotes

www.treasuryofquotes.com

Success Circle™
Monthly Interview Series

www.successcirclemonthly.com

Entrepreneurs, Small Business Owners, Self-Employed
Professionals, Salespeople and Others:

Are You Ready to Work Less, Make More Money
and Have More FUN?

Each month, Brian Bartes interviews entrepreneurs,
business leaders, authors and other experts who share
their most powerful tips, strategies and secrets for success.

In each interview, you'll discover:

- Real-world success stories of people who have built
  six- and seven-figure businesses . . . on their own terms.
- Personal success principles that will help you create
  the results you want faster, easier, and with greater
  predictability than you could on your own.
- Money-making strategies so you can increase your
  income without working more hours to do it.
- Mistakes to avoid along the way, saving you both time
  and money.

Whether you want to take your already successful business to the next level, or you're trying to get off the treadmill of stress and overwhelm, *Success Circle Monthly* will uncover specific strategies to help you achieve your desired outcome.

With each and every interview, you'll take away actionable, results-oriented ideas that will literally program you for success!

Once you experience the *Success Circle Monthly Interview Series* you'll be hooked by the tips, techniques and strategies to make more money in your business, AND have more time to enjoy your life.

For more information,
and to secure your **free 2-month trial membership,** go to:
www.successcirclemonthly.com